Recommended Methods for Range-wide Monitoring of Prairie Dogs in the United States

By Lyman L. McDonald, Thomas R. Stanley, David L. Otis, Dean E. Biggins, Patricia D. Stevens, John L. Koprowski, and Warren Ballard

Scientific Investigations Report 2011–5063

U.S. Department of the Interior
U.S. Geological Survey

U.S. Department of the Interior
KEN SALAZAR, Secretary

U.S. Geological Survey
Marcia K. McNutt, Director

U.S. Geological Survey, Reston, Virginia: 2011

For more information on the USGS—the Federal source for science about the Earth, its natural and living resources, natural hazards, and the environment, visit http://www.usgs.gov or call 1-888-ASK-USGS

For an overview of USGS information products, including maps, imagery, and publications, visit http://www.usgs.gov/pubprod

To order this and other USGS information products, visit http://store.usgs.gov

Suggested citation:
McDonald, L.L., Stanley, T.R., Otis, D.L., Biggins, D.E., Stevens, P.D., Koprowski, J.L., and Ballard, Warren, 2011, Recommended methods for range-wide monitoring of prairie dogs in the United States: U.S. Geological Survey Scientific Investigations Report 2011–5063, 36 p.

Contents

Table

Glossary of Abbreviations

ATV	All Terrain Vehicle
BTPD	Black-tailed prairie dog
CAS	Conservation Assessment and Strategy
CCM	Compressed county mosaics
CV	Coefficient of Variation
DOQQ	Digital ortho quarter quad tiles
ESA	Endangered Species Act
FSA	Farm Service Agency
GIS	Geographic Information System
GPS	Global Positioning System
GRTS	Generalized random tessellation stratified
GUPD	Gunnison's prairie dog
PDCT	Prairie dog conservation team
PVC	Polyvinyl Chloride
MSCP	Multi-State Conservation Plan
NAD	North American Datum
NAIP	National Agriculture Imagery Program
PSU	Primary Sampling Units
SRS	Simple random sampling
SSU	Secondary sampling units
USDA	U.S. Department of Agriculture
UTM	Universal Transverse Mercator
UTPD	Utah prairie dog
USFWS	U.S. Fish and Wildlife Service
USGS	U.S. Geological Survey
WAFWA	Western Association of Fish and Wildlife Agencies
WTPD	White-tailed prairie dog

Recommended Methods for Range-Wide Monitoring of Prairie Dogs in the United States

By Lyman L. McDonald,[1] Thomas R. Stanley,[2] David L. Otis,[3] Dean E. Biggins,[2] Patricia D. Stevens,[2] John L. Koprowski,[4] and Warren Ballard[5]

Overview

One of the greatest challenges for conserving grassland, prairie scrub, and shrub-steppe ecosystems is maintaining prairie dog populations across the landscape. Of the four species of prairie dogs found in the United States, the Utah prairie dog (*Cynomys parvidens*) is listed under the Endangered Species Act (ESA) as threatened, the Gunnison's prairie dog (*C. gunnisoni*) is a candidate for listing in a portion of its range, and the black-tailed prairie dog (*C. ludovicianus*) and white-tailed prairie dog (*C. leucurus*) have each been petitioned for listing at least once in recent history. Although the U.S. Fish and Wildlife Service (USFWS) determined listing is not warranted for either the black-tailed prairie dog or white-tailed prairie dog, the petitions and associated reviews demonstrated the need for the States to monitor and manage for self-sustaining populations. In response to these findings, a multi-State conservation effort was initiated for the nonlisted species which included the following proposed actions: (1) completing an assessment of each prairie dog species in each State, (2) developing a range-wide monitoring protocol for each species using a statistically valid sampling procedure that would allow comparable analyses across States, and (3) monitoring prairie dog status every 3–5 years depending upon the species. To date, each State has completed an assessment and currently is monitoring prairie dog status; however, for some species, the inconsistency in survey methodology has made it difficult to compare data year-to-year or State-to-State. At the Prairie Dog Conservation Team meeting held in November 2008, there was discussion regarding the use of

different methods to survey prairie dogs. A recommendation from this meeting was to convene a panel in a workshop-type forum and have the panel review the different methods being used and provide recommendations for range-wide monitoring protocols for each species of prairie dog. Consequently, the Western Association of Fish and Wildlife Agencies (WAFWA), in coordination with USFWS and U.S. Geological Survey (USGS), hosted a prairie dog species survey methodology workshop January 25–28, 2010 in Fort Collins, Colorado. The workshop provided all WAFWA partners and interested parties the opportunity to present their survey methodology to a review panel made up of experts in the fields of quantitative biology, population biology, species biology, and biostatistics. This report presents the panel's survey methodology recommendations for each of the four species of prairie dogs found in the United States and, for the black-tailed prairie dog, a list of action items to facilitate implementation of the recommended methodology.

Introduction

Background

In 1998, several nongovernmental organizations petitioned the USFWS requesting that the black-tailed prairie dog (BTPD) be listed as a threatened species under the ESA. In response to that petition, State wildlife agencies within the historical range of the BTPD formed the Black-tailed Prairie Dog Conservation Team and began discussions toward the development of an interstate effort to conserve the species. By November 1999, the Black-tailed Prairie Dog Conservation Assessment and Strategy (CAS; Van Pelt, 1999) was finalized that established a framework under which actions would be implemented to further conserve BTPDs within their historical range in the United States. Objectives of the CAS include establishing a prairie dog conservation team (PDCT), developing long-term conservation goals for the entire range of the BTPD (for example, determining the number of occupied acres and individual colonies or complexes of minimum size), identifying focal areas for conservation, developing survey

[1]WEST, Inc., 200 South Second Street, Laramie, WY 82070

[2]U.S. Geological Survey, Fort Collins Science Center, 2150 Centre Avenue, Building C, Fort Collins, CO 80526

[3]U.S. Geological Survey, Iowa Cooperative Fish and Wildlife Research Unit, Iowa State University, Ames, IA 50010

[4]Wildlife Conservation and Management, School of Natural Resources and the Environment, 306 Biological Sciences East, University of Arizona, Tucson, AZ 85721.

[5]Department of Natural Resources Management, Texas Tech University, Box 42215, Lubbock, TX 79409.

methods that would estimate occupied acres in each State and allow comparable analyses across States, preparing State specific management plans, and surveying the total number of occupied acres in each State at least once every 5 years. On February 4, 2000, the USFWS issued a finding of "warranted but precluded" (65 FR 5476), and the States continued to work on conservation measures.

In February 2003, the PDCT published an addendum to the CAS, entitled, "A Multi-State Conservation Plan for the Black-tailed Prairie Dog, *Cynomys ludovicianus*, in the United States" (MSCP; Luce, 2003). The MSCP provides further guidelines for achieving some of the objectives in the CAS and includes the following minimum 10-year target objectives (conservation goals) based on a range-wide analysis:

> "1) Maintain at least the currently occupied
>   acreage of BTPD in the U.S.
> 2) Increase to at least 1,693,695 acres of
>   occupied BTPD acreage in the U.S by
>   2011.
> 3) Maintain at least the current BTPD oc-
>   cupied acreage in the two complexes
>   greater than 5,000 acres that now occur
>   on and adjacent to Conata Basin-
>   Buffalo Gap National Grassland, South
>   Dakota and Thunder Basin National
>   Grassland, Wyoming.
> 4) Develop and maintain a minimum of
>   nine additional complexes greater than
>   5,000 acres (with each State managing
>   or contributing to at least one complex
>   greater than 5,000 acres) by 2011.
> 5) Maintain at least 10% of total occupied
>   acreage in colonies or complexes
>   greater than 1,000 acres by 2011.
> 6) Maintain distribution over at least 75%
>   of the counties in the historic range or
>   at least 75% of the historic geographic
>   distribution."

Initially, the Gunnison's prairie dog (GUPD) and the white-tailed prairie dog (WTPD) were not included in these efforts. However, in July 2002, a petition was filed to list the WTPD as endangered or threatened across its range. Subsequent to this filing, the BTPD Conservation Team (henceforth PDCT) was expanded to include both WTPDs and GUPDs because many of the same management issues, such as survey protocols, identification and ranking of threats, regulation changes, recreational shooting, management plan frameworks, relocation techniques, and long-term monitoring were similar for all three prairie dog species. In 2004, a petition was filed to list the GUPD under the ESA. Subsequently, conservation assessments were completed for both the GUPD (Seglund and others, 2005) and the WTPD (Seglund and others, 2006) evaluating the range-wide population status of each species and identifying factors limiting conservation. This was

followed by development of a White-tailed Prairie Dog and Gunnison's Prairie Dog Conservation Strategy (Western Association of Fish and Wildlife Agencies, 2006) which provided 9 conservation objectives with a number of specific conservation activities under each objective. One such conservation activity called for the evaluation and establishment of survey methods for monitoring GUPDs and WTPDs in each State that would allow for valid comparisons of results across States. A subsequent addendum (GUPD Conservation Plan; Western Association Fish and Wildlife Agencies, 2007) to this Conservation Strategy identified specific activities for GUPDs that would accomplish the objectives outlined in the Conservation Strategy. One of the goals of the GUPD Conservation Plan was to maintain occupied cells within at least 75 percent of a baseline number of geographical units within each State using a common protocol. The protocol proposed by Colorado and implemented by the other States within the range of GUPDs is known as occupancy sampling in modeled habitat. Using this protocol to monitor GUPD,s the States would identify a baseline occupancy rate and ultimately, for at least GUPDs, a trend over several sampling periods. It was determined by the PDCT that 700 plots would be sampled range-wide to detect occupancy trends in the GUPD population. In accordance with the GUPD Conservation Plan:

> "3. Actions (see below a.) will be triggered when/if a 40
>   % (95% CI) range-wide occupancy decline is detected
>   between surveys (i.e. 3 years; short-term trigger). A
>   long-term trigger for action will also be identified.
>   However, since process variation is unknown, this will
>   not take place until after 3 sample periods (i.e. 6 years)
>   have occurred. This timeframe will provide sufficient
>   data to identify a long-term trigger. This trigger will
>   be retroactive; if a certain percent decline is detected,
>   management actions will be initiated immediately.
>
> a. Actions Triggered: Within 1 year of reaching the
>   trigger, a course of action, on a state-by-state ba-
>   sis will be developed by the PDCT and presented
>   to WAFWA Directors for implementation. Though
>   the range-wide trend is being monitored, the spe-
>   cies may only be affected in distinct geographic
>   areas. However, all states will support actions
>   taken even if the area in decline is not within their
>   state boundaries. Support may include providing
>   funding or personnel.
>
> b. Surveys will be conducted annually until the trig-
>   ger is reset."

Currently, listing of the WTPD is not warranted (June 1, 2010; 75 FR 30338), and the GUPD is warranted for listing within the montane portion of its range (central and south-central Colorado and north-central New Mexico) however listing the montane GUPD is precluded by higher priority species and is therefore considered a candidate species (February 5, 2008; 73 FR 6660).

The Utah prairie dog (UTPD), found only in southwestern and central Utah, has been listed under the ESA since 1973, initially as endangered (June 4, 1973; 38 FR 14678), but downlisted to threatened on May 29, 1984 (49 FR 22330). The recovery criteria outlined in the Utah Prairie Dog Recovery Plan (United States Fish and Wildlife Service, 1991) are to establish and maintain the species as a self-sustaining viable unit with retention of 90 percent of its genetic diversity for 200 years. Activities proposed to accomplish this included:

"1. Establish and maintain one population each on public lands in three separate areas.

2. Maintain each population with a minimum number of 813 adult animals in the annual spring census."

A revised draft recovery plan recently was released for public review (September 17, 2010; 75 FR 57055), which when finalized, will likely establish new recovery criteria. Because we were already addressing three of the four species of prairie dogs found in the United States, WAFWA requested that we review the survey protocol for UTPDs, as well.

Current Status of Monitoring Efforts

Since 1999, many States have developed State-specific management plans and strategies towards achieving conservation goals. Prior to these efforts, prairie dogs themselves had not received much attention with regard to population inventory and monitoring and no systematic or consistent methods for managers were in use. Consequently, several methods have been developed for monitoring the prairie dog species found in each State (table 1). In 2006, all States within GUPD range agreed to use occupancy surveys and modeling, and several states began using this approach for WTPDs, as well. In addition to occupancy surveys and modeling, other current survey methodology ranges from aerial transects and ground surveys to use of satellite imagery. Not all methods provide repeatable, statistically accurate and precise estimates of the parameters of interest, nor are results comparable among States. This is especially true for BTPDs.

Purpose and Overview of the Prairie Dog Survey Methodology Workshop

In 2008, WAFWA recognized the States were devoting considerable effort and funding toward monitoring prairie dog populations; yet the methods used were inconsistent across States, and some methods were subject to criticism, especially for the BTPD. WAFWA also recognized that because of the different methodologies used, it was difficult to consolidate this information in a statistically rigorous manner to monitor progress towards achieving the target objectives as identified in the MSCP. In November 2008, after receiving a

recommendation from the PDCT, WAFWA and the USFWS requested assistance from the USGS in putting together a workshop to address this concern. Together WAFWA, the USFWS and the USGS organized a prairie dog survey methodology workshop in Fort Collins, Colorado, during January 25-28, 2010 (appendix 1). A panel of 6 experts in the field of quantitative biology, population biology, species biology, and biostatistics were appointed to review the current survey methodologies used by each State and for each species and to provide WAFWA with recommendations for standardization of survey methodologies for each species of prairie dog. Prior to the workshop, all twelve States were asked to respond to a set of questions regarding their survey objectives and methods (appendix 2) and provide any additional information they would like the panel to consider. Most States also provided oral presentations at the workshop. Additionally, one tribe and one nongovernmental organization provided written material and an oral presentation at the workshop. This report presents the panel's recommendations to standardize survey methodologies among the States for each of the four species of prairie dogs.

Basis for the Methods Recommended

The panel was asked to provide recommendations regarding suitable methodologies for assessing the status of each of the four species of prairie dogs occurring in the United States. Of these four species, the UTPD is listed as threatened, the GUPD is a candidate species (in at least a portion of its range) and the BTPD and WTPD have both been petitioned for listing under the ESA, although both were later determined not warranted for listing. For management purposes, there is a need for replicable monitoring methods capable of detecting presence of species, and in some cases at relatively low levels of abundance, throughout its range. Because listing decisions may be affected by the geographic distribution of species within their historical ranges, a monitoring method must be capable of providing spatially explicit information. For these purposes, the panel deemed it unnecessary to estimate numbers or densities of prairie dogs in areas where they are present. Rather, the panel judged that monitoring presence/absence of prairie dogs on land units, whether by occupancy modeling or estimation of occupied colony area, adequately addresses broad-scale status of prairie dog species. However, for the BTPD, additional information is required on number of occupied colonies of different sizes and the spatial distribution of occupied colonies (MSCP target objectives 3-6 above).

The panel's goal for all species was to suggest monitoring protocols that could produce statistically reliable estimates relevant to stated objectives in a cost-efficient and practical manner. Furthermore, the approaches that are recommended should provide significant "value-added" attributes that position the multi-State effort to respond effectively to changes in biological and economical conditions and maintain scientific rigor, based on the following principles:

Table 1. Summary of current methods used by States to monitor prairie dog populations.

[Estimated cost based on last survey conducted as noted in table, NAIP – National Agriculture Imagery, DOQQ – Digital Ortho Quarter Quad]

Species	State	Survey method	Last survey	Cost ($)
Black-tailed PD	Arizona	Ground survey	2010	13K
	Colorado	Aerial line transect with ground truthing	2006-2007	120K
	Kansas	NAIP imagery with aerial line transects	2009	17K
	Montana	Aerial line transects with ground truthing	2008	155K
	Nebraska	Aerial line transects and photos	2003	113K
	New Mexico	DOQQ imagery with ground truthing	2008	92K
	North Dakota	Aerial surveys with ground truthing	2006	48K
	Oklahoma	Aerial photos with ground truthing	2009	60K
	South Dakota	NAIP imagery with ground truthing	2008	31K
	Texas	DOQQ imagery with ground truthing	2006	82K
	Wyoming	NAIP imagery with aerial line transects	2009	15K
Gunnison's PD	Arizona (Aubrey Valley)	Block transects	2009	13K
	Arizona	Occupancy surveys and modeling	2008	26K
	Colorado	Occupancy surveys and modeling	2007	150-175K
	New Mexico	Occupancy surveys and modeling	2007	67.5K
	Utah	Occupancy surveys and modeling	2007	33K
White-tailed PD	Colorado	Occupancy surveys and modeling	2008	150-175K
	Montana	Mapping	2005-2008	6K
	Utah	Occupancy surveys and modeling with ground truthing	2008	44K
	Wyoming	NAIP imagery with aerial line transects	2008	20K
Utah PD	Utah	Mapped and counts of colonies	2009	23K

1. Techniques must be robust to fluctuations in State budgets in order to sustain the monitoring effort. The proposed methods must provide a reasonable approach, one that is conducive to advanced planning and budgeting by State agencies.

2. Techniques must be robust to changes in survey personnel over the years. While inter-observer differences in detection probabilities can be calculated and incorporated statistically as noted in the proposed methods, a common (multi-State) set of training materials for protocols should be considered.

3. Techniques must be comparable among States to satisfy requirements for range-wide data on occupied area and trends.

4. Data storage and availability in the face of changing State-agency management must be assured. A central data-storage host should be considered and a common Web-based interface for data entry might be pursued that would enable remote entry of data. These data would provide a critically important database for range-wide assessment of prairie dog species.

5. Techniques must be able to incorporate changing methods of analysis. In addition, with the innovations in digital imagery and the addition of bands such as near infrared, new analyses and reanalysis may become possible at the State or multi-State level.

6. Techniques must consider that changes on the landscape will occur due to changes in land-use patterns and climate change. The methods used must be able to incorporate the potential for changing distributions, loss of habitat patches and gain from restoration efforts. The proposed methods will permit change-detection methods (Lu and others. 2004; McDonald and others, 2009) to be applied on a large scale as another means of determining trends in land-use patterns, assessing global climate change impacts, and efficacy of restoration/preservation efforts.

7. Technique applications must clearly identify the methods used so as to allow replication in future years and by other States.

The subsequent sections of this report describe protocols that are consistent with these principles and can be used to monitor progress towards meeting the goals and objectives for BTPDs and the range-wide status of the other three prairie dog species. For the BTPD, we suggest that the use of an imagery-based sampling design coupled with aerial and/or ground-based assessment will be necessary to achieve all MSCP objectives. No single current State protocol satisfactorily achieves all of these objectives. In particular: (1) line-intercept methods cannot provide estimates of numbers of colonies in a given size class, (2) the accuracy of classified imagery should be evaluated rigorously by estimating detection probabilities using multiple observers, and (3) aerial surveys and photo interpretation alone cannot provide defendable estimates of the proportion of area occupied in a given colony, and therefore on-the-ground (ground) surveys must be completed. For WTPD and GUPD species, our assessment is that the current occupancy survey and modeling methodology is satisfactory for estimation of the proportion of occupied units; we provide several relatively minor suggestions for improvement. We recommend that the current UTPD monitoring program be modified to accommodate an occupancy survey and modeling methodology similar to WTPD and GUPD monitoring programs.

Lastly, although beyond the charge to the panel and not part of the panel's recommendations for this workshop, we think the use of conservation focal areas as discussed in the MSCP would be beneficial if extended to all four species of prairie dogs in the United States. Management and monitoring options on conservation focal areas should address questions of ecological functioning that will allow more refined goals to be set for future conservation efforts. For further discussion on the need for more concentrated effort on focal areas see appendix 3.

Survey Sampling Terminology

The terminology and definitions used in survey sampling are exact and are best described mathematically. However, because such formalism is beyond the scope of this document, we instead provide simple definitions of terms and concepts that will be referenced throughout this report. There are many valid alternatives in the design of a survey, each of which will require unique formulae for estimation of the total number of occupied acres of BTPDs and numbers of occupied units for WTPDs, GUPDs, and UTPDs. When possible, we give example formulae, however, it is impossible to give a complete set of possible designs, each with its unique formulae for expansion of summary statistics and estimation of associated variances, standard errors, and widths of confidence intervals. We recommend that a qualified statistician be consulted for each State to further derive and implement the necessary

formulae associated with whatever alternative design may be selected and developed.

Definitions

A *target population* is a set of units for which we wish to learn the value of some underlying *parameter*, where a parameter is a measurable quantity of interest. For example, in the present context, the set of all National Agriculture Imagery Program (NAIP; U.S. Department of Agriculture, 2009; appendix 4) images covering potential BTPD colonies in a State on June 1, 2010, might represent our target population. The total number of acres occupied by BTPDs might represent the primary *parameter of interest.*

In the special case where every unit of the target population (for example, every NAIP image) is assessed completely without error, we have a census, and the value of the parameter for the entire target population is determined without error. In most cases, however, it is not possible to census the target population and instead a sample of units must be drawn and the parameter estimated with some degree of error (that is, uncertainty). A sample is composed of a subset of the units from the target population and typically is drawn from a sampling frame. In its simplest form, a sampling frame is a complete list of the units in the target population. In the present example, the sampling frame would be the list of all NAIP images covering potential BTPD colonies on June 1, 2010. Given the sampling frame, a procedure, for example, simple random sampling (SRS) without replacement, is used to draw a sample from which inferences to the target population can be made. It is important to note that if the sampling frame is incomplete or inaccurate in some manner, for example, if some units that exist in the target population are omitted from the list, then inferences from the sample to the target population may be biased.

Recommendations

Black-tailed Prairie Dog Survey Methodology

General Comments and Action Items toward Developing a Range-Wide Survey Methodology

The panel was charged with reviewing existing BTPD monitoring methods used by the States, toward the goal of recommending a sampling and statistical framework allowing parameters of interest to be estimated in a rigorous and consistent manner among States. The panel has proposed such a framework for BTPD, as described in this report. However, to make that framework operational, it is necessary that the States and other interested parties take the next step to develop and collectively agree upon certain definitions and protocols.

Because many of these issues are not statistical in nature and lie outside the panel's realm of expertise or knowledge, we do not attempt to address them in more than general terms (for example, see the appendix). Rather, we believe the onus is on the States to develop definitions and protocols that are biologically meaningful, useful from a species management perspective, and practical and cost effective from an operational standpoint. We hasten to point out that, whereas many of these issues may benefit from the involvement of a statistician, ultimately they are management decisions and must be dealt with in a management framework. What follows is a list of action items that are necessary to move forward with implementing the monitoring framework proposed by the panel.

Action Item 1. States and other interested parties need to develop and agree upon a rigorous (that is, completely unambiguous), biologically meaningful, and formal definition of an "occupied acre" for BTPDs.

In preparing for this workshop the panel formed a set of "homework questions" that were forwarded to workshop participants in an effort to determine monitoring objectives. Clearly, it is not possible to develop a statistically valid monitoring framework if one does not know the objectives, or the end product desired. The first question posed was "What parameters are you trying to estimate?" (appendix 2). The answer to that question in the case of BTPDs was "occupied acres." Unfortunately, as the workshop progressed, it became evident that a formal and rigorous definition of occupied acres did not exist, and there was huge variation— conceptually and operationally— among participants with respect to what constituted an occupied acre. It is our opinion that the absence of an agreed-upon definition is hindering progress and creating unnecessary controversy, and that this will continue until a rigorous and formal definition is agreed upon.

It is not possible to specify a method or protocol for measuring a property of a system until that system property is defined unambiguously. In the case of the BTPD, one example of an unambiguous (but impractical) definition for occupied acres would be: the sum of the areas on which a prairie dog is currently standing (an area of a few square inches). Here there is no ambiguity as to whether the space is occupied, because a prairie dog (and not its burrow, set of burrow entrances, or clip line) is actually present, and there is no ambiguity with respect to area occupied because it is the space taken up by the prairie dog (not its burrow, some buffer around a burrow, or its clip line).

Unfortunately, in the case of the BTPD, occupied acres are often being measured—despite the absence of a definition—by drawing a subjective boundary around an indefinite collection of prairie dog burrows that may not even be currently occupied by prairie dogs. This, of course, leads to disagreements and controversy as to where the boundary should begin or end; how convoluted the boundary should be; whether a particular set of burrows (regardless of prairie dogs) should be considered one colony or two (or more); whether a 100-acre colony with a low density of prairie dogs should

be treated the same as a 100-acre colony with high density of prairie dogs; and whether part of a colony eliminated by poisoning should be included or excluded; and if excluded, where the boundary should be. The point is that you cannot know how to accurately and consistently measure occupied acres until you can define what occupied acres means.

Action Item 2. Convene a panel of experts to prepare written guidelines or other materials (for example, a set of example images) to train map interpreters on detecting potential prairie dog colonies (hereafter referred to as *features*) from NAIP imagery.

The panel did not possess the necessary expertise to produce rigorous guidelines or protocols on feature detection, thus we limited ourselves to suggesting items that should be considered (appendix 5). One reviewer of the draft of this document suggested a panel of statisticians, managers, imagery experts, and field personnel could be formed to develop and regularly review these guidelines. We agree with this sentiment and believe specific protocols should be developed and then used collectively by the States and other interested parties.

Action Item 3. Once Action Items 1 and 2 have been completed, formalize a set of guidelines on how to circumscribe features detected using NAIP imagery.

The value obtained for occupied acres depends on how the boundary around an area occupied by BTPDs is constructed and how areas within that boundary where burrows are absent (that is, internal structure) are circumscribed. Because construction of these boundaries may vary within and between map interpreters and may depend on the scale at which the images are viewed, the value obtained for occupied acres also will vary— even if the image of the occupied area does not change. The first step to resolving this problem is to complete Action Item 1 satisfactorily. Given an unambiguous definition of occupied acres, it should be possible to develop a formal standardized set of guidelines to deal with such issues as: (a) which scale should interpreters use; (b) time limit per image frame; (c) whether features should be circumscribed as one colony or multiple colonies; (d) determining where boundaries of colonies begin or end; (e) determining the boundaries around areas with low densities of burrows; or (f) delineating internal structure within colonies where burrows are absent. We note that how a BTPD colony should be circumscribed is not a statistical issue; it is an issue for the users of these data who need to decide what is meaningful from a biological, management, and policy perspective.

Action Item 4. Convene a panel of experts to prepare written guidelines or other materials to guide aerial surveyors on the classification of features as null, occupied, or unoccupied.

The estimated total acres of all features detected during photointerpretation is likely to be positively biased because some features circumscribed are not prairie dog colonies (that is, null features) and colonies may be completely or partially unoccupied. One of the sampling designs we propose to adjust for bias involves aerial surveys followed by ground surveys. Under some circumstances this design may be more efficient, statistically and from a cost perspective, than ground surveys only. During the aerial surveys, observers visit a set of randomly selected features identified during photointerpretation and classify each feature into one of three mutually exclusive categories: Null, Occupied, or Unoccupied. We suspect that aerial surveys will allow for definitive identification of null features (that is, features that are not prairie dog colonies), and sightings of prairie dogs will suffice as proof of occupancy (without estimating proportionate occupancy). Other attributes, for example, condition of burrows (are there open burrows?) and vegetation (is vegetation overgrowing the colony or the burrow entrances?) can provide evidence that a feature is not occupied by prairie dogs. The panel believes that it would be useful for representatives from States using aerial surveys to compile a list of attributes proven to be useful for classifying features as Null, Occupied, or Unoccupied from aircraft so as to guide surveyors classifying features.

Action Item 5 (optional). Evaluate the probability of detection of burrows and scat and correct classification of scat (that is, fresh or not) during ground surveys.

We provided an unambiguous definition of an occupied burrow based on presence of fresh scat within 0.5 m of a burrow opening as defined in appendix 6. Further, for purposes of ground surveys and subsequent analysis, we assumed that trained observers can consistently apply the definition of fresh scat; that detection of fresh scat (given that it exists within 0.5 m of a burrow) is approximately 100 percent; and the detection probability of occupied burrows and unoccupied burrows does not differ. Personnel from each State may want to evaluate whether these are valid assumptions through controlled studies.

Action Item 6. Representatives from each State should perform a cost analysis for the suitable suite of BTPD sampling procedures, so as to decide which procedures are most cost-effective for their State.

The panel developed the monitoring framework in a manner that allowed States some flexibility with respect to implementation, while still maintaining the elements necessary to ensure statistical rigor and consistency among States. We believed a fixed, inflexible "recipe" would be doomed to failure because different States must deal with certain unique issues, and clearly a one-size-fits-all approach is not practical. For example, some States may need to use aircraft, whereas others may find ground truthing adequate; some States may benefit from stratified random sampling, whereas for other States, simple random sampling (or some other sampling design) may be better; and for some States the desired level of precision may be attainable with smaller sample sizes, whereas other States may require larger sample sizes. Of course, each of these factors will affect the cost of monitoring,

as will personnel costs (for example, using permanent versus temporary staff), the size of the prairie dog range for a State (larger ranges mean more travel costs), the proportion of the range that is on public versus private land (more private land means higher personnel costs to contact landowners), the desired statistical precision, and so forth. In short, the costs of implementing the monitoring framework we propose will be unique for each State and will vary depending on the particular implementation chosen for that State. Thus, it is important that representatives for each State examine their unique set of circumstances, decide on the sets of procedures available to them to implement the monitoring framework for their State, and then determine the respective costs for implementation so they can choose the most cost-effective approach.

Action Item 7 (optional). Retain the services of a statistician to formally critique one or more of the State-specific methods currently being used to monitor prairie dogs, relative to the MSCP objectives (for BTPDs) and/or any State-specific objectives.

The panel was not charged with providing a State-by-State critical review of the methodology being used. The panel's goal was to become familiar with the multiple approaches being used in each State, to become informed with respect to the challenges personnel in each State must confront, and then to propose a consistent and statistically rigorous framework within which all States could operate (with some built in flexibility for unique circumstances). Our expectation was that individual States could ascertain the strengths and weaknesses of their existing protocol by comparing it to the Panel's recommendations. We would note that for certain sets of objectives many of the methods presented by States were adequate from a statistical standpoint. However, at least for BTPDs, none of the methods in use was 100 percent adequate with respect to either meeting the stated MSCP objectives or statistical rigor. Hence, we proposed an alternative framework we believe is adequate. If States have certain sets of objectives that differ from those the panel was charged with addressing, then we urge them to have their methods reviewed by a qualified statistician.

Action Item 8. The panel believes the sixth MSCP objective *"maintain distribution over at least 75% of the counties in the historic range or at least 75% of the historic geographic distribution"* needs to be better articulated and made more explicit before an appropriate sampling design can be recommended.

As it currently stands, the sixth objective is ambiguous and does not lend itself to the development of formal, standardized sampling procedures. Specifically, three tasks must be completed: (1) make explicit what is meant by "*maintain distribution*", (2) list the counties that are considered to be in the historic range, and (3) explicate what is meant by "*at least 75 % of the historic geographic distribution.*" We elaborate further on these tasks, and provide illustrative examples, in the section below titled Estimation of the Proportion of Counties in the Historic Range that Contain BTPD.

Parameters of Interest

Measuring progress towards meeting the Target Objectives outlined in the MSCP requires knowledge of the currently occupied acreage of BTPDs in the United States. For purposes of developing a standardized monitoring program among States, the *primary parameter of interest* for the BTPD is the number of occupied acres of BTPD as summarized by each State at some specified point in time as described in MSCP Objectives 1-2. Additional parameters of interest include the number and locations of large (that is, 1,000-5,000 acre) colonies or complexes in order to gauge progress towards meeting the MSCP Objectives 3-5 and to maintain 75 percent of the historic distribution as described by MSCP Objective 6 . For purposes of discussion, we hereafter assume that: (1) the BTPD range in the United States can be represented by a mutually agreed upon (that is, among States and other stakeholders), static (that is, unchanging through time), spatially explicit area of land; (2) what constitutes an "active burrow" can be rigorously and unambiguously defined (see appendix F); and (3) the occupied acres within a colony can be estimated in a biologically meaningful and replicable manner (however, see Action Items 1-4). In the discussion below we describe a methodology geared toward estimation of "occupied acres" that is founded upon these assumptions.

Target Population

For the BTPD monitoring program, the primary parameter of interest is the number of occupied acres of BTPD existing in the United States at some specified point in time. Thus, in principal, our target population should include the set of all occupied acres of BTPD in the United States at some point in time. However, because this set is dynamic over short time frames and in practice is unobservable (for example, existence and location of some colonies is unknown), we instead define the *target population* to be the collection of digital images that encompasses all geographic areas lying within the current, historical, and potential range of the BTPD. The target population is divided into a set of discrete sampling units. The definition of the target population we adopt is useful because an appropriate sampling frame can be easily constructed (for example, using NAIP imagery, see below), and because correction factors for partially unoccupied colonies within the range can be estimated.

With respect to current range, we believe it is important to include all lands on which BTPD are currently known to reside because the status of those colonies must be taken into account in the event of a petition for listing. Categorically excluding certain occupied lands will result in a negatively biased estimate of occupied acres and will unnecessarily open the monitoring effort to valid criticism. The implication here,

of including all areas where BTPD currently reside, means private land, metropolitan, Tribal, military and other Federal land, and arbitrarily excluded land in prior surveys must be considered part of the range containing the target population subject to sampling in each State.

With respect to historical range, we presuppose that if records exist documenting the presence of BTPDs in an area prior to widespread extermination or conversion of grasslands to other uses (for example, agriculture), then there is a possibility the area can be recolonized in the event extermination is halted or grasslands reclaim the area. Consequently, such areas should be included as part of the range containing the target population subject to sampling. Assessment of the historical range for all prairie dog species should include evaluation of Federal, State, and County records of attempts to eradicate prairie dogs. County agricultural extension agents, State and Federal biologists, conservation wardens, and others could provide valuable information on locations of remnant populations in the 1940s and 1950s.

Finally, with respect to the potential range of the BTPD, we recommend representatives in each State predict the expanded range that could be occupied, under favorable future conditions, by using a 100-year time horizon. Consideration should be given to potential changes in the landscape due to factors, such as fire, which may kill shrubby vegetation, allowing for the establishment of grasslands; clearing of woody vegetation, which might allow for expansion of grasslands; and changes in grazing of vegetation by herbivores. One implication here is that State models containing current vegetation conditions as predictor (independent) variables to delineate BTPD range should be modified to eliminate vegetation variables, and instead use features that will remain static during the next 100 years (for example, elevation, slope, soils).

Specifying the target population. The current, historical, and potential range for BTPDs must be identified for each State. The union of these areas across States will be considered the range containing the target population for which BTPD occupied acres will be estimated. Estimates of occupied acres will not apply to any land area outside of this range. Once the target population has been defined, it should not change so as not to invalidate comparisons of occupied acres over time.

Sampling Frame and Image Analysis

Constructing the sampling frame. Once the BTPD range has been delineated, the sampling frame for each State is constructed by acquiring, for example, current NAIP imagery (appendix 4) for the entire portion of the BTPD range occurring within the State. Each NAIP image (or a merged set of images of arbitrary but constant size) represents a sample unit, and collectively these units comprise the *sampling frame*. Units overlapping the boundary of the BTPD range should be clipped to exclude portions of the units lying outside of the range. Other sources of remotely sensed images can be used if they contain sufficient detail for observers to identify potential

BTPD colonies (that is, features). Furthermore, we recognize that technology for remote sensing of the earth's surface will change in the future, and hence, the units comprising the sampling frame may change through time. We believe the protocols recommended below are robust to such changes. For simplicity, we hereafter assume that NAIP images will be used to construct the sampling frame.

Feature identification. For the first year of the monitoring program we recommend that every unit in the State's sampling frame (BTPD range) be examined independently by two skilled interpreters, each of whom will identify and circumscribe features without reference to any pre-existing data on the locations of known prairie dog colonies. See Action Items 1-3 and appendix 5 for more details on the use of aerial imagery to classify and map features. The purpose of using multiple independent interpreters is twofold.

First, using multiple interpreters makes it possible to construct a "capture history" for each feature that is detected, so that the number of features not detected by any interpreter can be estimated. Specifically, suppose there are two interpreters. If interpreter A detects a particular feature (denoted by a '1') and interpreter B does not detect that particular feature (denoted by a '0'), then the capture history for that feature is {1 0}. Likewise, {0 1} denotes a feature not detected by interpreter A that was detected by interpreter B, and a {1 1} capture history denotes a feature detected by both interpreters. In cases where one interpreter merged features that the other interpreter split, the interpreters will need to reconcile their differences and mutually agree to either merge or split the features. These features will have a {1 1} capture history. This capture-history information, pooled for all features detected by at least one interpreter, forms a capture-history matrix that can be used under the Huggins (1991) model in Program MARK (White and Burnham, 1999; White, 2008) or Package MRA (Analysis of Mark-Recapture data, Amstrup and others, 2005, p. 241-245; McDonald, 2010) to estimate the number of features not detected by either interpreter. Because the Huggins (1991) model allows detectability to be modeled as a function of covariates, it will be possible to use the size, s =area of features (in acres), and interpreter identification (to account for detection differences of interpreters) as covariates to model probability of detection. Estimation under appropriate models and use of these software packages is not a trivial exercise. Again, we emphasize the need for consultation with a qualified statistician to assist with model development and analysis.

The second reason for using multiple independent interpreters is to provide a more robust estimate of the size of features and to facilitate discussion and standardization of rules for delineation of boundaries (see Action Items 1-3 above). However, we anticipate that the measurement error associated with circumscribing a feature will be small compared to the variation in sizes of all features detected and that it can be ignored, assuming that there is no significant positive or negative bias. Guidelines and tips for identifying, circumscribing, and preclassifying features on NAIP imagery are provided in appendix 5.

In the event that the individual detection probability of features is high (for example, >0.95) during the first year that

the survey protocol is implemented and the variation among interpreters in circumscribing features is low, it should be possible to use only one experienced interpreter to develop the sampling frame from the new NAIP imagery during subsequent years. We envision a scenario in which a GIS layer containing the locations and outlines of features identified in the preceding survey, are overlaid onto the NAIP imagery for the current survey and used as a guide for locating and circumscribing expanding, shrinking or new features (that is, potential new BTPD colonies or BTPD colonies missed the first time). However, if individual detection probability of features is low, or in subsequent years new interpreters are used, we recommend continued use of two independent interpreters. In subsequent years where two interpreters are used, a capture-history matrix for new features (only) could be constructed to estimate the number of new features not detected by any interpreter.

Feature analysis. Let N denote the number of sampling units (NAIP images) comprising the sampling frame within a State, and suppose every sample unit in the frame is viewed independently by interpreters A and B. Let m denote the total number of features detected by interpreters A and B (collectively). Denote the estimated probability of detection of the ith feature by interpreter A by $\hat{p}_{ai}$, $i = 1, 2, 3, ..., m$, where it is understood that this estimate may depend on the size of the ith feature, s_i, (in acres) and other covariates. We assume that the measured size of the feature is the average of the measured sizes recorded by interpreters A and B. We also assume that measurement error for the size of a unit is small compared to variation of sizes among features and can be ignored. Similarly, denote the estimated probability of detection of the ith feature by interpreter B by $\hat{p}_{bi}$, $i = 1, 2, 3, ..., m$. As noted above, models for estimating detection probabilities can be constructed using the Huggins model for analysis of mark-recapture data (Huggins, 1991).

Assuming independence among interpreters, the estimated probability that the ith feature of size s_i will be missed by both interpreters is $\hat{p}_i = (1 - \hat{p}_{ai})(1 - \hat{p}_{bi})$, and the estimated probability it will be detected by at least one interpreter is $\hat{\pi}_i = 1 - \hat{p}_i$. Given the set of m features detected, an estimate of the total number of features in the sampling frame of units (NAIP images), M, is given by the Horvitz-Thompson estimator (Horvitz and Thompson, 1952):

$$\hat{M} = \sum_{i=1}^{m} \frac{1}{\hat{\pi}_i} . \tag{1}$$

The estimated total acres, $\hat{S}$, of all features in the sampling frame of units is:

$$\hat{S} = \sum_{i=1}^{m} \frac{s_i}{\hat{\pi}_i}. \tag{2}$$

The estimated number of features missed by both interpreters A and B is given by $\hat{M} - m$, and the estimated total acres of features missed is $\hat{S} - \sum_{i=1}^{m} s_i$.

If only a random sample of n units from the population of N units is examined, then the sample statistics $\hat{S}$, $\hat{M} - m$, and $\hat{S} - \sum_{i=1}^{m} s_i$ should be divided by the sampling fraction n/N to account for the units not surveyed. Variances of statistics would be estimated by standard, but fairly complex, explicit formulae from the theory of sampling with unequal probability without replacement, if the divisors in equations (1) and (2) were known constants. Estimated variances would be reduced by the finite sampling fraction $(1 - n/N)$. More complicated sample survey designs will require unique and sometimes complex adjustments. However, in this case, the divisors in (1) and (2) are themselves estimates from the Huggins model for analysis of mark-recapture statistics (Huggins, 1991). For this reason, we recommend use of a computer intensive resampling procedure known as bootstrapping for estimation of variances, standard errors, and limits of confidence intervals (Manly, 2006) taking into account the complete estimation process including air- and ground-survey exercises (see the Estimation of variances, standard errors, and confidence interval limits section below).

Survey Sampling Designs for Field Efforts

The estimated total acres of all features in the sampling frame, $\hat{S}$, is a positively biased estimate of occupied acres due to 2 factors: (1) some features in the sampling frame are not prairie dog colonies, and (2) colonies may be completely or partially unoccupied. Hence, our estimate of S must be adjusted by factors correcting for these biases to first estimate the proportion of features that are prairie dog colonies and then to estimate the proportion of the colonies that are occupied. We now describe two alternative sampling designs for collecting data to correct for these biases. In the first design, an aerial survey is used to assign each feature to 1 of 3 status categories: Null (not a prairie dog colony), Unoccupied, or Occupied. This stratification of all features then provides a framework for selection of a subsample of colonies for use in a ground survey to estimate the proportion of the colony that is occupied. In the second design, only a ground survey is completed. Both designs will result in estimates of the total area occupied by BTPD in the State.

Method 1. Aerial Survey then Ground Survey
The primary purpose of the aerial survey is to increase the cost-efficiency of the subsequent ground survey (see Action Item 6). None of the features assigned Null status will be included in the ground survey and therefore we assume that assignment of features to this category is done without error. A sample of features to be ground-surveyed is taken from both the Occupied and Unoccupied categories. These 2 samples are selected independently. We suggest that a much larger proportion of features be selected from the Occupied category, because we assume that features assigned to this category in the aerial survey will represent the majority of total occupied acres in the State. However, it is important to select a reasonable sample from the Unoccupied category as well, because we do not assume that the aerial survey assignment

to Unoccupied or Occupied status is without error. Thus, our philosophy is to use the aerial survey to maximize efficiency of ground surveys by: (1) eliminating features that are not colonies, and (2) allocating the majority of ground-survey resources to colonies we believe to be occupied. It is important to note that the subsequent estimates of occupied acres derived from the ground survey are not biased by errors in assignment to occupied or unoccupied status in the aerial survey.

Aerial survey then ground survey—aerial survey design. The collection of m features identified by interpretation of the NAIP imagery will constitute a second sampling frame for aerial and ground surveys. However, some features may be in "no-fly" zones (for example, on military bases or in cities) and cannot be aerially surveyed, and for other features it may not be possible to gain access for ground surveys (for example, access to features on private land may be denied). Inaccessible features selected for sampling should be labeled as "missing data."

For ease of presentation, much of the following notation and formulae assume no spatial stratification. However, we envision that each State may stratify its range of BTPD spatially, ranging from relatively high density of features to low density. For example, the BTPD range in South Dakota might include a "low density" stratum on the east side of the Missouri River. If spatial stratification is used, the same notation and formulae can be applied to each stratum in a straightforward manner.

To keep the notation simple, assume that an aerial census of features is completed and all m features that were identified from NAIP imagery in the office are classified during the aerial survey into Occupied BTPD colonies (m_O), Unoccupied BTPD colonies (m_U), and features that are not BTPD colonies (m_{null}). Based on the aerial classification, the Horvitz-Thompson estimate of total acres of features,

$$\hat{S} = \sum_{i=1}^{m} \frac{s_i}{\hat{\pi}_i},$$

can be divided into three separate estimates: (1) an estimate of the total acres of aerially classified Occupied BTPD colonies (including features missed by both interpreter A and B in the office) is

$$\hat{S}_O = \sum_{i=1}^{m_O} \frac{s_{Oi}}{\hat{\pi}_{Oi}},$$

where s_{Oi} is the size of the ith occupied feature and $\hat{\pi}_{Oi}$ is the estimated probability of detection of the ith occupied feature; (2) similarly, the total acres of aerially classified Unoccupied BTPD colonies would be estimated by

$$\hat{S}_U = \sum_{i=1}^{m_U} \frac{s_{Ui}}{\hat{\pi}_{Ui}};$$

and (3) the balance is the estimate of acres of features that are not BTPD colonies, where $\hat{\pi}_{Oi}$ and $\hat{\pi}_{Ui}$ are the same probabilities of detection estimated under the Huggins (1991) model from the photo-interpretation exercise with two independent interpreters. If only one interpreter is used, $\hat{\pi}_{Oi}$ and $\hat{\pi}_{Ui}$ are assumed to equal 1.

An aerial census of all features may not be economically possible or the precision of a census may not be required for making desired inferences. We suggest two possible methods for selecting a sample of features to be aerially surveyed, although we acknowledge that many other valid sampling schemes could be used. If the probability of detection of features during double sampling of NAIP images is high, particularly for small features, then it may be reasonable to assume a simple random sample of m_1 features is unbiased. In this case, the first and simplest statistically valid protocol would be to choose a simple random sample offeatures from the sampling frame of all m features (or those features within a stratum). However, we would recommend a generalized random tessellation stratified (GRTS) spatially balanced sample of m_1 features (Stevens and Olsen, 2003, 2004; McDonald, 2004). After the m_1 features are mapped, it may be economically possible to fly to each and classify them as Occupied, Unoccupied, or Null. All features assigned Null status are assumed to contain no prairie dogs and are therefore, excluded from further analysis and surveys. Aerial surveys of features also will enable determination of the degree of misclassification of other features as prairie dog colonies during the photo-interpretation process (false positives).

Denote the number classified as occupied by m_{1O} and the number classified as unoccupied by m_{1U}. The probability that a feature will be detected in the office and selected for aerial survey (then classified as occupied during the aerial survey) is the product of the probabilities $(m_1 / m) \hat{\pi}_{Oi}$. An estimate of the total acres of aerially classified occupied BTPD colonies is then

$$\hat{S}_O = \sum_{i=1}^{m_{1O}} \frac{s_{Oi}}{(m_1/m)\hat{\pi}_{Oi}} = \left[\frac{m}{m_1}\right] \sum_{i=1}^{m_{1O}} \frac{s_{Oi}}{\hat{\pi}_{Oi}},$$

where the sum is over the m_{1O} occupied features detected. Similarly, the estimate of the total acres of aerially classified unoccupied BTPD colonies is

$$\hat{S}_U = \left[\frac{m}{m_1}\right] \sum_{i=1}^{m_{1U}} \frac{s_{Ui}}{\hat{\pi}_{Ui}}.$$

However, we expect that completely random selection or GRTS sampling of features within a State or within large strata may be biased because small features are under-represented, or because it may not be cost-efficient owing to the increased time and cost incurred by having to fly to individual random locations to survey a single feature. Therefore, we next describe an alternative cluster sampling design that may be more cost-effective for many States.

Using a cluster sampling framework, a new 'Sampling Frame' of Primary Sampling Units (PSUs) could be defined as strips or some other group of images of a fixed size that can be surveyed economically from an airplane. Let Q be the total number of PSUs. For cost-efficiency, PSU sizes should be large compared to the size of most BTPD colonies, for example, size of PSUs might be selected so that the majority of PSUs are expected to contain at least 10 features. The set of delineated features within each PSU constitute the secondary sampling units (SSUs).

The next step is to select a probabilistic sample of PSUs from the State or from each stratum. Suppose a simple random or GRTS sample of 'Q_1' PSUs is selected and that all features (SSUs) within each selected PSU are surveyed aerially. Each feature (SSU) in each selected PSU is assigned a status as Occupied, Unoccupied or Null. Note that the entire image area represented by the PSU is not being surveyed. Only features previously identified and delineated in the office will be checked. All SSUs assigned Null status will be excluded from further analysis and will not be included in the ground survey sampling frame.

Features bisected by the boundary of a PSU require special attention. To preserve desired statistical properties of the estimate of area occupied, we need an objective decision rule for inclusion of a bisected feature in the sample. Our suggestion is to assign each feature to the PSU that contains its centroid. This point can be easily generated during GIS image analysis, and it unambiguously assigns each feature to a unique PSU and avoids the potential for size-bias in the sample.

Denote the number of features classified as occupied by m_{1O} and the number classified as unoccupied by m_{1U}. The probability that a feature will be detected in the office and selected for aerial survey (then classified as occupied during the aerial survey) is the product of the probabilities $(Q_1 / Q)\hat{\pi}_{Oi}$. An estimate of the total acres of aerially classified, occupied BTPD colonies is

$$\hat{S}_O = \sum_{i=1}^{m_{1O}} \frac{s_{Oi}}{(Q_1/Q)\hat{\pi}_{Oi}} = \left[\frac{Q}{Q_1}\right] \sum_{i=1}^{m_{1O}} \frac{s_{Oi}}{\hat{\pi}_{Oi}},$$

where the sum is over the m_{1O} occupied features detected. Similarly, the estimate of the total acres of aerially classified unoccupied BTPD colonies is

$$\hat{S}_U = \left[\frac{Q}{Q_1}\right] \sum_{i=1}^{m_{1U}} \frac{s_{Ui}}{\hat{\pi}_{Ui}}.$$

We suggest sampling a total of 50 PSUs with about 8 SSUs in each PSU in the first year of design. A total of approximately $n=50\times8=400$ features surveyed is expected to yield estimates of simple proportions with half-width of a 95 percent confidence interval $<(1/\sqrt{n})=0.05=5$ percent for the proportions of features in the categories (Occupied, Unoccupied, Null). The rationale for the numbers 50 and 8 is not strong because the estimates are not simple proportions; however the authors judge that these sample sizes will produce estimates within about ±5 percent of their true values with 95-percent confidence. As will be the case with most of the sample-size recommendations made in this report, it is difficult to rigorously derive sample sizes expected to achieve a statistical objective (for example, precision) absent prior experience and estimates of relative costs inherent in the sampling design. Our expectation is that data generated from an initial survey will be used to improve the efficiency of future surveys.

More complicated survey designs will require unique adjustment factors. Discussion of estimation of variances and confidence limits is postponed until after adjustment of statistics derived from ground surveys.

Aerial then ground survey—ground survey design. Recall that the objective of the ground survey is to produce estimates of the average proportion of area occupied in colonies. An important issue in the design of the ground survey is whether to include colonies classified as "Unoccupied" in the aerial survey. We might reasonably expect that the number of occupied acres estimated from ground surveys of aerially classified "Unoccupied" BTPD colonies would be negligible compared to the total estimate of occupied acres, but this assumption could bring the entire survey into question. Thus we recommend sampling "Unoccupied" colonies but with a reduced sampling effort.

The set of Occupied and Unoccupied colonies identified in the aerial survey constitutes the sampling frame for the ground survey. As discussed above, selection of colonies for ground survey could be achieved by a simple random sample within each of the Occupied and Unoccupied strata. However, we recommend a GRTS spatially balanced sample (Stevens and Olsen, 2003, 2004) so as to better account for any large-scale spatial patterns in occupancy. In the event that a selected colony cannot be accessed, the colony would be listed as missing data and the next colony on the GRTS list will be considered the alternative. This includes inaccessible colonies on military land, tribal land, and other private land. The GRTS procedure will rank order all features in the State or stratum. The first features on the GRTS list serve as the original sample, and the remaining features are alternates in the order listed.

Alternatively, if a cluster sampling approach is preferred, a random sample of PSUs is selected, and within each selected PSU a random sample of SSUs is chosen. Within each sampled PSU, Occupied colonies should be classified into 2 size classes, such as, relatively large (for example, >10 acres) and relatively small. Definition of large and small may vary from State to State, but should be coordinated among States; however, the idea is that relatively more ground survey effort will be expended on relatively large colonies. We suggest that 24 of the 50 PSUs sampled in the aerial survey be chosen randomly. If the State has been stratified geographically, a minimum of six PSUs should be selected from each stratum. A GRTS spatially balanced sample (Stevens and Olsen, 2003, 2004) of sample size 2 will be selected from each of the two size classes and surveyed for estimation of the proportion of occupied acres. Thus, we are recommending a minimum total of 96 (=24×2×2) Occupied colonies be selected for ground surveys. For Unoccupied colonies within a selected PSU, a GRTS spatially balanced sample of sample size 2 is selected. Thus, we are recommending a minimum total 48 (=24×2) Unoccupied colonies be sampled.

These recommended total sample sizes of 96 and 48 also apply if individual colonies are chosen using the previously described GRTS spatially balanced selection procedure.

Colonies selected for the ground survey and for which access cannot be obtained are to be labeled as "missing data" and the rate of missing data should be reported. This includes inaccessible colonies on military land, tribal land, and other private land. In the event that a selected colony cannot be accessed, the next colony on the GRTS list will be considered the alternative. The GRTS procedure will rank order all SSUs in each stratum of the PSU. The first two on the GRTS list serve as the original sample, the third is the first alternate if data on one of the first two is missing, the fourth is the second alternate, and so forth. If colonies labeled as "missing data" are systematically different than colonies in general (for example, they are poisoned more or less frequently), then we would expect some unknown bias to occur in our estimates of occupied acres.

We anticipate that the results from the initial survey completed in each State under this protocol will be used to modify the above recommended sample sizes based upon achieved and desired precision of the estimates.

Method 2. Ground-Only Survey Design

The ground-only survey design has the advantage that estimates of occupied area are made for every sampled feature, and sources of sampling error associated with aerial survey classification are eliminated. However, the available sampling frame is based only on the original delineation of features from the NAIP imagery. Thus, if features are selected by a simple random sample, or stratified random sample based on size of features, Occupied, Unoccupied, and Null features would have equal probabilities of selection, which most likely would lead to inefficient use of ground survey time. This is a major disadvantage of the ground-only survey design option, but we recognize that some States may not wish to do aerial surveys.

We suggest that all features in the sampling frame be stratified into large and small categories, as previously described. The sampling effort is then weighted heavily toward the larger features, with smaller (but non-zero) weights assigned to the smaller features. Assume there are m_S features in the "small" stratum and m_L units in the "large" stratum. The estimated total acres of features identified by equation (2),

$$\hat{S} = \sum_{i=1}^{m} \frac{s_i}{\hat{\pi}_i},$$

is divided into two components, $\hat{S} = \hat{S}_S + \hat{S}_L$, where

$$\hat{S}_S = \sum_{i=1}^{m_S} \frac{s_{iS}}{\hat{\pi}_{iS}}, \text{ and } \hat{S}_L = \sum_{i=1}^{m_L} \frac{s_{iL}}{\hat{\pi}_{iL}}.$$

However, each of these estimates includes acreage of Null features and therefore the formulae need to be adjusted for this positive bias. We assume that the first step in the ground survey protocol described in the next section will be to do an assessment of the feature to determine if it is Null (not a colony). Let p_S and p_L be the proportion of Null features in the large and small strata as determined from this rapid assessment. Then the adjusted estimates are

$$\hat{S}_S = (1 - p_S)\sum_{i=1}^{m_S} \frac{s_{iS}}{\hat{\pi}_{iS}} \text{ and } \hat{S}_L = (1 - p_L)\sum_{i=1}^{m_L} \frac{s_{iL}}{\hat{\pi}_{iL}}.$$

As with the prior design, our goal is to achieve a representative sample of colonies to be surveyed on the ground by using a probabilistic sampling protocol. The simplest protocol would again be to select individual colonies completely at random from the sampling frame. We believe this protocol would not be cost-efficient and therefore we again suggest an alternative 2-stage random-selection protocol to increase efficiency. At the first stage we select a sample of PSUs exactly as described in the previous design. At the second stage, instead of sampling all SSUs within each selected PSU, we select a simple random sample from each of the two size-class strata. We suggest selection of 50 PSUs and 8 SSUs per PSU, with an overall objective of sampling about 400 features. A total of 400 features is expected to yield estimates of simple proportions with half-width of a 95-percent confidence interval $<(1/\sqrt{n})=0.05=5$ percent for the proportions of features in the categories (Occupied, Unoccupied, Null). The rationale for the numbers 400, 50 and 8 is not strong because the estimates are not simple proportions; however the authors judge that these sample sizes will produce estimates within about ± 5 percent of their true values with 95-percent confidence. Again, regarding the sample size recommendations made in this report, it is difficult to rigorously derive sample sizes without an explicitly stated statistical objective (for example, precision) absent prior experience and estimates of relative costs inherent in the sampling design. Our expectation is that data generated from an initial survey will be used to improve the efficiency, and if necessary, to modify sample sizes in future surveys.

Ground Survey Sampling Protocol

The purpose of the ground survey is to estimate the proportion of the colony area, as circumscribed by using NAIP imagery, that is occupied, or equivalently, the proportion not occupied (for example, due to plague or poisoning). However, this is problematic because there does not seem to be any rigorous, formal definition of an occupied acre (see Action Item 1 above). Instead, we have a subjective boundary drawn around a collection of prairie dog burrows that may or may not be occupied by prairie dogs. Because the acreage of the area contained within the colony boundary is positively biased (with respect to occupied area) in situations where, for example, plague or poisoning of prairie dogs has recently occurred, it is necessary to adjust that acreage downward. But development of a formal correction factor requires a rigorous definition of "occupied". At one extreme we might decide that the only area occupied in the colony is that on which a prairie dog is currently standing, an area of a few square inches. On the

other extreme, we might define a square mile to be occupied if at least one live prairie dog is detected within the boundaries. Or we might conceptualize the amount of occupied acres in a colony as the sum total of all active home ranges of individuals within the colony boundary, then define an average home range area, and consider a sampled plot of the area as occupied if it contains at least one active burrow. Another method would exclude empty burrows, any buffers around the margin of the colony (for example, clip line area), and sum the areas of certain size buffers around active burrows. Alternatively, we might define a set of active (that is, containing at least one living prairie dog) burrows, where no burrow is more than 5 meters from at least one other burrow in the set, as a 'home range' cluster that we can circumscribe (for example, using the minimum convex polygon method), and the area contained within that boundary represents "occupied area." Then the occupied area for the colony would be the sum of these cluster areas.

Development of a definition for occupied acres is not a statistical problem that can be solved by the panel. Rather, it is a problem for the users of the results of this monitoring framework to confront. The users must decide on a definition that ideally is both biologically meaningful and easily measurable in the field. Given an unambiguous definition of occupied acres, the panel, or others, can suggest an estimation technique.

Despite the absence of a definition for occupied acres, the panel reasoned that colony boundaries exist for no other reason than that they contain prairie dog burrows. If there were no burrows there would be no colony boundary, hence no occupied acres. Furthermore, we realized each burrow can exist in one of two states: it is occupied occasionally by at least one prairie dog or it is not. Thus it is possible, in principle, to determine the proportion of occupied burrows contained within the colony boundary. Because a colony with zero occupied burrows is definitely unoccupied and therefore has zero occupied acres, and because a colony where every burrow is occupied is definitely a fully occupied colony and all of the acreage should be considered as occupied, we concluded that a reasonable estimate of occupied acres for a colony is the number of acres in the colony multiplied by the proportion of burrows that are occupied (we are not attempting to estimate prairie dog density or abundance). Thus, estimation of occupied acres collapses to the problem of estimating the proportion of occupied burrows in the colony.

We propose using strip transects to subsample non-null features (i.e., the sample units) during ground surveys for purposes of estimating the proportion of occupied burrows. We suggest an unambiguous definition of an occupied burrow based on presence of fresh scat within 0.5 m of a burrow opening as defined in appendix 6. We also assume that trained observers can consistently apply the definition of fresh scat, that detection of fresh scat (given that it exists within 0.5 m of a burrow) is approximately 100 percent, and detection probability of occupied burrows and unoccupied burrows does not differ. States may want to evaluate whether these are valid assumptions (see Action Item 5).

In all cases, a transect should begin and end at the edge of a colony, and there must be at least two transects. The first transect should be placed a random distance from and parallel to the major axis of the colony, and the second transect should be placed a random distance from and parallel to the minor axis of the colony (imagine an ellipse). Technically, the strips are primary sampling units and the correct estimate of sampling variance is variation among strips; however, the authors judge that development of a stopping rule based on variation among strips is too tedious to implement in the field. In its place, we recommend an approximation based on the assumption that the burrows examined are a reasonable representation of a simple random sample of burrows. Under this assumption, 200 burrows would yield an approximate 95-percent confidence interval on the proportion of occupied burrows with half-width $<1/\sqrt{200}=7$ percent. Precision for a stratum is expected to be better than ± 7 percent when data are pooled across surveyed colonies. Additional transects, parallel to and at random distances (these should be spatially balanced random distances) from either axis, should be added if the total number of burrows classified (that is, the denominator in the formula for R below) on both transects is less than 200. Once a total of 200 burrows have been encountered, no additional transects need be added, though the two mandatory transects mentioned above still must be completed. If there are fewer than 200 burrows in a colony, then every burrow should be examined to determine the proportion of occupied burrows. We recommend specifying transect beginning and ending points (that is, their GPS coordinates) in the office, prior to going into the field where subtle biases might be inadvertently introduced. Features should be visited between 1 June–30 September.

Each BTPD burrow encountered in the surveyed strip transect will be classified as Occupied or Unoccupied following the protocol outlined in appendix 6. The area searched will be the length times the width of the strip transect(s), hence density of occupied and density of unoccupied burrows can be computed for each sampled feature. In addition, States may elect to record UTM coordinates of encountered BTPD burrows, in which case, spatial arrangement of burrows within features can be mapped and studied. However, these metrics do not easily transform into estimates of "occupied acres" as discussed above. We recommended that the metric used to standardize estimates of occupied acres across States and strata within States be defined by the product of the estimated proportion of occupied burrows and the estimated size of the occupied colonies. For a given stratum, denote the estimated proportion of occupied burrows by

$$\hat{R} = \frac{T_O}{T_O + T_U},$$

where T_O and T_U are the total observed number of occupied and unoccupied BTPD burrows, respectively, in all colonies in the ground survey in the stratum. From the above, the total acres

of colonies in the stratum are estimated by $\hat{S}$. We recommend the estimator for "occupied acres" of BTPD, O, in the stratum be the product $\hat{O}_{acres} = \hat{R} \times \hat{S}$. We recommend that standard errors of estimates and confidence intervals be obtained by bootstrapping the data, because there are no explicit formulas for computation (see the "Estimation of variances, standard errors, and confidence interval limits" section below).

For example, if the total acres of aerially classified occupied colonies in the northeast corner of Kansas was estimated to be 10,000, and the proportion of occupied burrows in ground surveyed aerially classified occupied colonies in northeast Kansas is 0.6=60 percent, then the estimated number of occupied acres of BTPD in aerially classified occupied features of northeast Kansas is 6,000 acres. For ease of presentation, subscripts have been dropped from some of these formulae. If features within a spatial stratum have been substratified into further strata, for example, large and small features or occupied and unoccupied features, then estimates of occupied acres within the spatial stratum, for example, the northeast corner of Kansas, will be totaled to obtain the estimated total number of occupied acres for the spatial stratum.

We recognize the need to compare and sum the estimates of occupied acres of BTPD across States. Beginning in 2009, the NAIP program committed to a 3-year cycle of acquisition so that all States would be guaranteed regular coverage conducive to planning and budget. The NAIP images will likely not be available at the same time for all States, in which case it may be necessary to add estimated acres from three consecutive years; for example, the survey in Kansas may be done in 2012, the survey in Nebraska may be done in 2013, and the survey in Arizona may be done in 2014. Regardless of the obvious objections, we see no alternative to adding the estimates for occupied acres for future reports involving several States.

Estimation of Occupied Acres in Large BTPD Complexes

The third objective in the MSCP prescribes, "*maintain at least the current BTPD occupied acreage in the two complexes greater than 5,000 acres that now occur on and adjacent to Conata Basis-Buffalo Gap national Grassland, South Dakota and Thunder Basin National Grassland, Wyoming.*" For these 2 large complexes, we recommend circumscribing any features that might be associated with these complexes by using the most recent NAIP imagery available and by using the criteria developed under Action Item 3 (see also appendix 5). Next, the perimeters of the complexes formed by these features must be established. This is accomplished by connecting the outer boundaries of colonies that are separated by ≤7 km (7 km rule) as described in detail in appendix 5. Once the boundaries of a complex have been established, the set of features contained within the complex boundaries constitute a sampling frame that is then subject to the BTPD sampling methods described above. Briefly recapping, a sample of features (or perhaps all of the features if there are not too many) are randomly selected and then sampled using Method 1 (aerial survey followed by a ground survey) or Method 2 (ground-only survey design). As already described, features selected for sampling are first classified as Null, Occupied, or Unoccupied, and then a sample of these are subject to the ground survey sampling protocol used to estimate the ratio (R) of occupied burrows to all burrows. Formulae presented earlier in this document are then applied to estimate occupied acres within the complex, and this can be used to determine if occupied acres on the 5,000+ acre complexes are being maintained.

The fourth objective in the MSCP prescribes, "*Develop and maintain a minimum of nine additional complexes greater than 5,000 acres (with each State managing or contributing to at least one complex greater than 5,000 acres) by 2011.*" The fifth objective prescribes, "*Maintain at least 10% of total occupied acreage in colonies or complexes greater than 1,000 acres by 2011.*" For the nine additional 5,000+ acre complexes described in Objective 4 and the 1,000+ acre complexes described in Objective 5, we recommend that potential 5,000+ or 1,000+ acre complexes previously known or newly identified from examination of NAIP imagery be handled similarly to the 5,000+ acre complexes described in the previous paragraph (for Objective 3). As noted above, features (potential colonies) that might be associated with the complexes will be circumscribed and then the complex boundaries will be established by using the 7 km rule (see appendix 5). Whereas Objectives 4 and 5 do not explicitly state that the 5,000+ or 1,000+ acres in these complexes must all be "occupied acres", if we assume for the moment this was the intent then it is necessary to proceed as described for Objective 3 above: draw a random sample of features from the complex, survey the features using *Method 1* or *Method 2*, then follow up with the ground-survey sampling protocol to estimate R. Apply the formulae presented earlier in this document to estimate occupied acres.

Under Objective 5, in order to estimate if 10 percent of the total occupied acreage in colonies or complexes greater than 1,000 acres is reached and/or maintained, the first step would be to sum occupied acres estimated for the 1,000+ and 5,000+ acreage complexes, as described in the previous two paragraphs. The second step would be to compute the total occupied acres for 1,000+ acre features already (incidentally) sampled by the States—because they were randomly selected for sampling to determine total occupied acres for their State—and add this total number of occupied acres to the sum obtained for the complexes (call this sum *s*). Finally, divide this new sum *s* by the estimated total occupied acres across the entire BTPD range (that is, across all States). If this value is greater than or equal to 0.1, then Objective 5 has been met and no additional sampling will be needed. However, if this proportion is < 0.1 then additional sampling of features greater than 1,000 acres is necessary. To accomplish this, identify the set of all features (not complexes) > 1,000 acres in size and remove from this set all features that have already been sampled. The set of features that remains forms a sampling

frame that can be handled as described above: draw a random sample of features from the complex, survey the features using *Method 1* or *Method 2*, follow up with the ground survey sampling protocol to estimate *R*, then apply formulae to estimate occupied acres. Add the estimated occupied acres to the sum *s* for complexes and 1,000+ acre features already sampled, then divide this new sum by the estimated total occupied acres across the entire BTPD range (i.e., across all States). If this value is greater than or equal to 0.1, then Objective 5 has been met.

Estimation of the Proportion of Counties in the Historic Range that Contain BTPD

The sixth MSCP objective is to "*maintain distribution over at least 75% of the counties in the historic range or at least 75% of the historic geographic distribution.*" The panel believes this objective needs to be better articulated and made more explicit before an appropriate sampling design can be recommended, and therefore we have listed it as an action item earlier in the report (see Action Item 8 above). Under this action item three tasks must be completed.

The first task is to make explicit what is meant by "maintain distribution." For example, if we pick a particular county known to be in the historic range then we can suppose that, historically, it contained at least one prairie dog, and perhaps many prairie dogs organized into one colony, many colonies, or even a mix of colonies and complexes. So, what do we mean when we ask the question "has the distribution been maintained in this county"? Do we mean that, presently, there is at least 1 prairie dog in the county, at least one colony in the county, at least one complex in the county, or that the number of occupied acres in the county is greater than or equal to the "historic" number of occupied acres in the county? The panel cannot recommend a sampling design to assess whether the distribution has been maintained until we know what exactly is meant by maintaining the distribution.

The second task is to list the counties that are considered to be in the historic range. In particular, it is important to know whether areas covered by these counties are a proper subset of the BTPD range specified under the guidelines we provided earlier in this document. Additionally, it will be important to know if there exists one or more counties included in the current BTPD range that are counties not considered part of the historic range.

The third task is to explicate what is meant by "at least 75% of the historic geographic distribution." As presented, there are multiple ways to interpret this. For example, is the historic geographic distribution some contiguous area containing a fixed number of acres? If so, then all we need to do is estimate occupied acres for this fixed area and see if it is greater than 75 percent of the area. Alternatively, is the historic geographic distribution some known set of historic colonies for which the area is known? If so, then all we need to do is estimate the area of overlap between the historic colonies and the present day colonies and determine if the overlap is at least 75 percent. Another possible meaning for historic geographic distribution might be some fixed set of colonies that can be enumerated. So, for example, there may be 137 historic colonies, so all we have to do is determine how many of those historic colonies contain at least one prairie dog and calculate whether 75 percent of the historic colonies contain at least one prairie dog.

Clearly an appropriate sampling design cannot be developed for this objective until all of these tasks are completed.

Estimation of Variances, Standard Errors, and Confidence Interval Limits

Computing the estimated variance (standard errors) of occupied acres is complicated by the fact that models are used for estimation of detection probabilities in equations (1) and (2). Alternative survey designs exist for aerial and ground surveys. Unknown biases may be introduced with missing data and limited access to some air and ground space. For these reasons, it will be difficult or impossible to derive explicit formulae for the standard errors of final estimates of occupied acres of BTPD colonies (Buckland and others, 2009).

We recommend that following the first survey in a State, estimates of standard errors and confidence intervals be obtained by bootstrapping the sample data based on the survey design used and the associated statistical methods as closely as possible, recognizing some potential for bias due to lack of access to all potential habitat. Bootstrapping involves resampling of all data sets (with simple random sampling and replacement) and reanalysis, including fitting of intermediate models, at each step to adequately represent total variation in the final statistics (Manly, 2006). We note that GRTS spatially balanced samples and systematic samples are expected to have less sampling variance than simple random samples (Stevens and Olsen, 2003, 2004; Manly, 2009). This implies that if data are collected by systematic sampling or GRTS spatially balanced sampling from a study area (State, County, stratum, and so on), then bootstrapped statistics using simple random sampling with replacement are expected to exhibit conservative (too large) estimates of variance of the original statistics. That is, confidence intervals obtained by bootstrapping systematic or GRTS samples are expected to be a little wider than the nominal confidence interval, but are still useful for assessing sampling variation.

Idealized steps in the bootstrapping process are outlined in the following paragraphs and will likely require the participation of a statistician to complete because field and analysis methods may be slightly different in States or in strata within States.

Step 1. The panel has recommended a complete census of all images in the office for identification of features that may contain BTPD. Let m denote the total number of features detected by interpreters A and B (collectively). Select a simple random sample without replacement of size m, that is, a

bootstrap sample of size m. Refit the Huggins model to obtain bootstrap estimates of

$$\hat{\pi}_i = 1 - \hat{p}_i \text{ and } \hat{S} = \sum_{i=1}^{m} \frac{s_i}{\hat{\pi}_i} \text{ (equation 2).}$$

If a random sample of n units (images) from the population of N units (images) is examined, then a bootstrap sample of the n units would be obtained to yield a bootstrap sample of features detected and bootstrap estimates of

$$\hat{\pi}_i = 1 - \hat{p}_i \text{ and } \hat{S} = \sum_{i=1}^{m} \frac{s_i}{\hat{\pi}_i}.$$

Step 2. The panel suggested several alternative approaches to adjust

$$\hat{S} = \sum_{i=1}^{m} \frac{s_i}{\hat{\pi}_i}$$

using either aerial surveys followed by ground surveys or ground only surveys using equal probability sampling at each step (simple random samples, systematic samples, GRTS samples, simple random samples within strata, and so forth). Resample the data sets with replacement and repeat the same estimation and adjustment methods to obtain bootstrap estimates of whatever statistics were originally obtained. For example, obtain bootstrap estimates of acreages of aerially classified Occupied and Unoccupied BTPD colonies $\hat{S}_O$ and $\hat{S}_U$, if the protocol for aerial surveys followed by ground surveys was used.

Step 3. Resample with replacement the burrows examined by the ground-survey sampling protocol to obtain a bootstrap estimate of the estimated proportion of occupied burrows

$$\hat{R} = \frac{T_O}{T_O + T_U},$$

for each stratum or subset under consideration.

Step 4. Obtain the bootstrap estimate of occupied acres, $\hat{O}_{acres} = \hat{R} \times \hat{S}$, for each stratum or subset under consideration. Sum the estimates over all strata or subsets to obtain the bootstrap estimate of total occupied acres.

Step 5. Repeat steps 1 through 4 a large number of times, for example, 1,000 times, to obtain 1,000 or more bootstrapped estimates of total occupied acres.

Step 6. Compute, for example, the standard deviation of the 1,000 bootstrapped estimates to obtain an estimate of the standard error of the total occupied acres. Report, for example, the 2.5th and 97.5th percentiles to obtain an approximate 95-percent confidence interval on the total occupied acres.

If double sampling of units (NAIP images) with independent interpreters in the office is judged not to be necessary in the second or future surveys, then it may be possible to estimate standard errors and confidence intervals by using explicit formulae from classical finite-sampling theory and eliminate the need for bootstrapping of variances and confidence limits.

Assessing the Effects of Lag Time

We acknowledge the issue of the potential bias in estimates because of a lag time between the date of the NAIP photography and the date of the ground survey. Based on current estimates of NAIP turnaround time and previous experience of States that have used NAIP imagery in their current survey protocols, we assume the lag between the two would be one year. A drastic decrease in the status of a colony due to poisoning or disease could occur during this year-long interval. However, this phenomenon does not result in positive bias because the estimates pertain to the number of occupied acres on the date of the ground survey, not the date of NAIP photography. Alternatively, negative bias in the estimates could result from the development of new colonies after the NAIP photography date because these colonies would not be included in the sampling frame for the ground surveys and the expansion factors applied to the surveyed sites would be too small. However, we suggest that the contribution of occupied acres from these new colonies (<1 year old) would represent a relatively negligible contribution to the overall total estimate.

White-tailed Prairie Dog and Gunnison Prairie Dog Survey Methodology

Parameters of Interest

Because of the difficulty of detecting and circumscribing WTPD and GUPD colonies in some States (for example, due to vegetation and indefinite boundaries), we recommend the parameter of interest for WTPDs and GUPDs be the proportion of occupied units throughout their range (MacKenzie and others, 2006; Andelt and others, 2009) rather than the number of occupied acres. The statistical theory and application for estimation of the proportion of occupied units in a target population has been well-developed and described by MacKenzie and others (2006), and we refer analysts to this publication for details. Our proposed methodology generally is equivalent to the approach used by Andelt and others (2009) in Colorado. We note that occupancy models also enable estimation of the probability an unoccupied unit will become occupied (colonization) and the probability an occupied unit will become unoccupied (extinction). The critical feature of these models is the estimation of detection probability, often as a function of measurable covariates. Detection probability is defined as the probability that a prairie dog is detected on a single survey visit to a sampling unit, given at least one prairie dog is present on the unit. Estimation of this nuisance parameter is made possible by a sampling design that requires multiple independent surveys of each sampled colony. We note that although it may seem logical to multiply the estimated proportion of occupied units in the range by the number of acres in the range to estimate total occupied acres, this calculation is inappropriate because the area of each occupied unit is not

necessarily completely occupied. Thus, under the methodology we describe, a defensible estimate of total occupied acres is not possible.

For purposes of discussion, we hereafter assume that: (1) the WTPD and GUPD "range" in the United States can be represented by a mutually agreed upon (that is, among States and other stakeholders), static (that is, unchanging through time), spatially explicit area of land; and (2) the definition of an occupied sampling unit is rigorously and unambiguously described (for example, visual detection of at least one living prairie dog within the boundaries of the unit).

Target Population

The primary parameter of interest in the monitoring program is the proportion of occupied units throughout WTPD or GUPD range. We define the target population to be the geographic area that encompasses the complete range of WTPDs or GUPDs. This geographic area, hereafter referred to as just "range", includes all areas lying within the current, historical, and potential geographic range of WTPDs or GUPDs in the United States.

With respect to current range, we believe it is important to include all land on which WTPDs or GUPDs are currently known to reside because the status of the land must be taken into account in the event of a petition for listing or reviewing current candidate listings. Categorically excluding certain land areas may result in a biased estimate of occupancy (positive or negative) and will unnecessarily subject the monitoring effort to valid criticism. The implication of including all areas where WTPDs or GUPDs currently reside is that metropolitan, Tribal, military and other Federal land, and other arbitrarily excluded land must be considered part of the range containing the target population subject to sampling by State personnel.

With respect to historical range, we presuppose that if records exist documenting the presence of WTPDs or GUPDs in an area prior to widespread extermination or conversion of habitat to other uses, then there is a possibility that the area can be recolonized in the event extermination is halted or habitat is restored to the area. Consequently, such areas should be included in the target population.

Finally, with respect to the potential range of WTPDs or GUPDs, we recommend each State predict the expanded area that could be occupied, under favorable conditions, using a 100-year time horizon. Consideration should be given to potential changes in the landscape due to factors such as fire or clearing of vegetation. One implication here is that States using models that contain current vegetation conditions as predictor (independent) variables to delineate WTPD or GUPD range should modify their models in favor of models using variables that will remain static during the next 100 years (for example, elevation, slope, soils).

Each State must identify the current, historical, and potential range for WTPDs and GUPDs. The union of these areas will be considered the entire species range. Estimates of occupancy will not apply to any land area outside of this range. We assume that each State will independently estimate the proportion of occupied units within its boundaries. An estimate of occupancy for the entire range can be obtained by calculating a weighted average of State estimates, where the weights are the relative sizes of ranges within each State.

Sampling Frame and Sampling Design

Constructing the sampling frame. The sampling frame is constructed by placing a grid of 500 by 500 meter units over the range delineated for WTPDs or GUPDs and assigning a unique identifier to each unit. For the sake of consistency and size of units, we recommend that the entire unit be included in the range if the boundary of the unit intersects the original range map.

Sampling Design. If the units comprising the frame are not stratified in any manner, then a simple random sample, or preferably a spatially balanced random sample (for example, see Theobald et al. 2007) can be drawn. A stratified random sample also could be drawn, perhaps using a spatially balanced random sample within strata. Thereafter, for early detection of trend in occupancy rates, we recommend revisiting these same units during each future survey effort. However, we recommend: (1) minimizing the number of strata to keep sample-size requirements reasonable, (2) stratifying by using criteria that can be determined a priori (no poststratification), and (3) ensuring units are unambiguously and permanently assigned to strata.

MacKenzie and others (2006) provide extensive recommendations for determination of sample size, which in this case involves both the number of units sampled and the number of surveys per unit. Sample sizes will depend on the desired statistical objective and assumed values for detection probability and probability of occupancy. As an example, suppose that our statistical objective is a 5 percent standard error for the estimate of proportion of occupied units. Based on results in Andelt and others (2009), we assume a probability of detection of 0.7 and an expected proportion occupied of 0.25. These values result in a recommendation of ~100 sampled units and 2 surveys per unit. We encourage all States contained in the range of each species to discuss establishment of a statistical objective for the monitoring program, for example, a desired precision of the occupancy proportion estimate, or a desired power to detect a specified change in occupancy rates over some time horizon (Andelt and others, 2009). This objective can then be used to refine required sample sizes for the number of sampled units to be monitored.

Sampling Plan, Data Collection, and Parameter Estimation

All surveys of the units selected for sampling to determine occupancy status should be completed during the following periods: WTPD, 1 March-15 July; GUPD, 15 Apr-15 Aug. A unit is considered occupied only if at least one living prairie dog is sighted by an observer within the boundaries of the unit; otherwise, the unit should be considered unoccupied. In most cases this will entail ground surveys by independent observers, with visits spaced far enough apart in time to minimize the effects of unusual weather, but close enough in time to ensure the closure assumption of the underlying model is met. A good source describing specific survey methods is Andelt and others (2009). An alternative monitoring design could involve using two independent aerial surveys of sampled units.

With two independent observations, a two occasion capture history of 0s (denoting unoccupied) and 1s (denoting occupied) can be constructed and analyzed using the methodology of MacKenzie and others (2006). Standard operating procedures for field surveys should maintain constant probability of detection of an occupied unit, to the extent possible, for example, by requiring that surveys only be conducted during certain daylight hours, weather conditions and with experienced observers. Covariates (weather, observer experience, and so on) can, however, be used to model detectability or occupancy, and these should be collected for every unit surveyed and every observer surveying the unit.

Utah Prairie Dog Survey Methodology

Parameter of Interest

We agree that the "Utah prairie dog occupancy and habitat survey protocol for Federal section 7 consultations" (U.S. Fish and Wildlife Service, 2010) is adequate for Federal Section 7 Consultations. However, we do not believe that the protocol is adequate to monitor UTPDs over a 100-year time horizon. The dispersion of UTPDs on the landscape seems similar to dispersion of other members of the white-tailed subgenus. Colonies with sufficient density and size to be outlined on maps are interspersed with scattered colonies at lower densities. We recommend the parameter of interest for long-term monitoring of UTPD be the proportion of occupied units throughout their range (MacKenzie and others, 2006; Andelt and others, 2009) by using the same methodology recommended for survey of WTPDs and GUPDs. Under our proposed methodology, it also would be possible to estimate the probability that an unoccupied unit will become occupied (colonization) and an occupied unit would become unoccupied (extinction). For purposes of discussion, we hereafter assume that: (1) UTPD "range" can be represented by a mutually agreed upon, static (that is, unchanging through time), spatially explicit area of land; and (2) what constitutes an occupied sampling unit can be rigorously and unambiguously defined (that is, visual detection of at least one UTPD within the boundaries of the unit).

Target Population

The primary parameter of interest in this monitoring program is the proportion of occupied units throughout the UTPD range. We define the target population to be the geographic area that encompasses all occupied units of UTPDs. The geographic area, hereafter referred to as "range", includes all areas lying within the current, historical, and potential geographic range of UTPDs in the United States.

With respect to current range, we believe it is important to include all land on which UTPDs are currently known to reside, (that is, metropolitan, Indian, military and other Federal land). With respect to historical range, we presuppose that if records exist documenting the presence of UTPDs in an area prior to widespread extermination or conversion of habitat to other uses, then there is a possibility the area can be recolonized in the event extermination is halted or habitat is restored to the area. Consequently, such areas should be included as part of the range containing the target population subject to sampling.

Finally, we recommend that the potential range of UTPDs be estimated including land where the species might someday occur, under favorable conditions, by using a 100-year time horizon. Here consideration should be given to potential changes in the landscape due to factors such as, fire, change in land use, or clearing of vegetation. One implication here is that States that use models containing current vegetation conditions as predictor (independent) variables to delineate UTPD range should modify their models in favor of models using variables that will remain static during the next 100 years (for example, elevation, slope, soils). The union of the current, historical, and potential range will be considered the range containing the target population for which UTPD occupancy will be estimated. Estimates of occupancy will not apply to any land area outside of this range.

Sampling Frame and Sampling Design

Constructing the sampling frame. The sampling frame is constructed by placing a grid of 500 by 500 meter units over the range delineated for UTPDs and assigning a unique identifier to each unit. For the sake of consistency and size of units, we recommend that the entire unit be included in the range if the boundary of the unit intersects the original range map.

Sampling Design. If the units comprising the frame are not stratified in any manner, then a simple random sample, or preferably a spatially balanced random sample (for example, see Theobald and others, 2007), can be drawn. A stratified random sample also could be drawn, perhaps using a spatially balanced random sample within strata. Thereafter, for early detection of trend in occupancy rates, we recommend revisiting these same units during each future survey effort. However, we recommend: (1) minimizing the number of strata to keep sample size requirements reasonable, (2) stratifying by using criteria that can be determined a priori (no

poststratification), and (3) ensuring units are unambiguously and permanently assigned to strata.

All surveys of the units selected for sampling to determine occupancy status should be completed during 15 Apr-15 Aug. For recommendations regarding sample sizes, refer to the discussion in the White-tailed Prairie Dog and Gunnison's Prairie Dog Survey Methodology section.

We encourage Utah to discuss establishment of a statistical objective for the monitoring program.

Sampling Plan, Data Collection, and Parameter Estimation

Refer to recommendations in the White-tailed Prairie Dog and Gunnison's Prairie Dog Survey Methodology section.

Concluding Remarks

In this report, we provide recommendations for a sampling and statistical framework that can be used to monitor progress towards meeting the goals and objectives for BTPDs and the range-wide status of the other three species (WTPDs, GUPDs, and UTPDs) found in the United States. In developing our recommendations, we recognized the difficulty of monitoring each species of prairie dog over large geographic areas, in highly variable habitat, and for three of the species, in multiple states. We also recognized that although our recommendations provide a framework for monitoring the status of each prairie dog species, there will continue to be a need for more intensive research and monitoring programs to provide more in-depth biological information to address the individual conservation and management needs of each prairie dog species.

With respect to BTPDs, we believe that our recommendations provide a workable framework allowing the parameter of interest, occupied acres, to be estimated in a rigorous and consistent manner, and allowing the comparison of data across years within States and among States. This approach allows for flexibility in the approach taken, is consistent with what we believe is the historical view of an 'occupied acre', and also allows use of remote sensing and aerial survey methods in States with large expanses of ground to cover, or with a high proportion of private land where access issues make strict ground-survey methods difficult. Overall, the six MSCP Objectives for the BTPD did not lend themselves to one simple, clean, elegant sampling design. Whereas MSCP Objectives 1 and 2 are well handled by the proposed design, achieving MSCP Objectives 3-5 may require additional effort and sampling. Likewise, the inherent ambiguity of MSCP Objective 6 did not allow us to address this objective in the proposed sampling framework at this time. Refinement of this objective, along the lines described in Action Item 8, will be required before this objective can be retrofitted into the proposed framework. More generally, we believe much work remains to be done by the States to agree collectively upon certain definitions and protocols as suggested in the list of action items we have provided. We believe these issues must be resolved in order to move forward with successful implementation of the monitoring framework proposed.

With respect to WTPDs and GUPDs, the objectives emphasize documenting presence or absence with the purpose of detecting changes. Perhaps the thinking regarding conservation of these species has not yet evolved to the point of considering focal complexes of colonies exceeding 1,000 or 5,000 acres and/or conservation of communities of prairie dogs and their associates (aside from those complexes that have received reintroductions of black-footed ferrets). Given this simplicity and lack of guidance from a multistate conservation plan similar to that for the BTPD, our recommendation to use the numbers of occupied 500 by 500 meter units as the parameters of interest for WTPDs and GUPDs rather than the numbers of 'occupied acres' was a fairly easy decision. This approach has been used successfully for GUPDs across the range and is well described in the literature. Given the objectives, we believe this approach is adequate for long-term monitoring of each species when measured over their full potential ranges.

Regarding the GUPD specifically, the panel cautions the States that the short-term trigger [40 percent (95 percent CI) range-wide occupancy decline between subsequent surveys] identified in the GUPD Conservation Plan (Western Association of Fish and Wildlife Agencies, 2007) might fail to identify a slowly declining trend (<40 percent) in occupancy, to the point that the species could be monitored to a critically low level without "triggering" an action. The proposed development of the long-term trigger in the next year or two should include a threshold that is based on some fixed percentage (with a set level of precision for the estimate) from a baseline value in order to prevent a decline that fails to trigger an action.

The UTPD is unique from the other species because of its present status as threatened under the ESA. Because of this, monitoring seemingly has been much more intensive for UTPDs than for the other two member of the subgenus (WTPD and GUPD), but the panel was not comfortable that the methods used would provide statistically defensible assessments of status. Because some of the problems of monitoring UTPDs are similar to those encountered with monitoring WTPDs and GUPDs (for example, low densities of prairie dogs in shrub-steppe habitats), the panel concluded that the methods based on occupancy models and described for WTPDs and GUPDs would work equally well for UTPDs. Nevertheless, objectives that will be listed in the upcoming revision of the recovery plan may require the addition of other types of monitoring that can assess densities of UTPDs and doubtless will require other conservation measures (see appendix 3).

Finally, the panel puts forth one additional remark. The proposed sampling framework, for all species, embodies the core elements necessary to launch a successful, statistically sound monitoring program. However, in many places specific details on implementation have been left out because certain facets of this program have never been tried before, or have alternative methods for implementation; therefore, we do not currently know the best implementation. Consequently, it is incumbent upon the States to mutually develop and agree upon standard operating procedures for implementing the program and to share successes and failures so improvements can be made during subsequent iterations of the survey. Flexibility, creativity, ingenuity, and communication among the States will be crucial for success.

Acknowledgments

We would like to acknowledge the contributions of numerous individuals in the completion of this report. Bill Van Pelt, Western Association of Fish and Wildlife Agencies, who approached U.S. Geological Survey with the idea of conducting a workshop and providing a report on recommended range-wide monitoring protocols, and provided valuable guidance throughout the process. Pete Gober, U.S. Fish and Wildlife Service, who along with Bill, recognized the need for standardization of prairie dog monitoring protocols and requested assistance from U.S. Geological Survey. Jeffrey Green, U.S. Animal and Plant Health Inspection Services, kindly provided workshop facilities. Michael Hutchins, The Wildlife Society, provided workshop opening comments on the role science plays in management decisions, political arenas, and public perception. Lee Lamb, Negotiation Guidance Associates, provided workshop facilitation and moderation. Laura Ellison, U.S. Geological Survey, provided workshop media support. Steve Sheriff and Brian Cade provided helpful reviews of the draft final version of the report. And finally, all the workshop presenters and participants who offered their time, expertise, comments and suggestions throughout all phases of this project.

References Cited

Amstrup, S.C., McDonald, T.L., and Manly, B.F.J., eds., 2005, Handbook of capture-recapture analysis: Princeton, New Jersey, Princeton University Press.

Andelt, W.F., White, G.C., Schnurr, P.M., and Navo, K.W., 2009, Occupancy of random plots by white-tailed and Gunnison's prairie dogs: Journal of Wildlife Management, v. 73, p. 35–44.

Barnes, A.M., 1993, A review of plague and its relevance to prairie dog populations and the black-footed ferret, *in* Oldemeyer, J., Biggins, D., Miller, B., and Crete, R., eds., Management of prairie dog complexes for reintroduction of the black-footed ferret: Washington, D.C., U.S. Fish and Wildlife Service, Biological Report 13, p. 28–37.

Biggins, D.E., and Kosoy, M.Y., 2001, Influences of introduced plague on North American mammals: implications from ecology of plague in Asia: Journal of Mammalogy, v. 82, p. 906–916.

Biggins, D.E., Godbey, J.L., Gage, K.L., Carter, L.G., and Montenieri, J.A., 2010, Vector control improves survival of three species of prairie dogs (*Cynomys*) in areas considered enzootic for plague: Vector-Borne and Zoonotic Diseases, v. 10, no. 1, p. 17–26.

Biggins, D., Miller, B., Hanebury, L., Oakleaf, R., Farmer, A., Crete, R., and Dood, A., 1993, A technique for evaluating black-footed ferret habitat, *in* Oldemeyer, J., Biggins, D., Miller, B., and Crete, R., eds., Management of prairie dog complexes for reintroduction of the black-footed ferret: Washington, D.C., U.S. Fish and Wildlife Service, Biological Report 13, p. 73–88.

Biggins, D.E., Sidle, J.G., Seery, D.B., and Ernst, A.E., 2006, Estimating the abundance of prairie dogs, *in* Hoogland, J.L., ed., Conservation of the black-tailed prairie dog: Washington, D.C., Island Press, p. 94–107.

Buckland, S.T., Russell, R.E. , Dickson, B.G., Saab, V.A., Gorman, D.N., and Block, W.M., 2009, Analyzing designed experiments in distance sampling: Journal of Agricultural, Biological, and Environmental Statistics, v. 14, no. 4, p. 432–442.

Chipault, J.G, 2010, Fine-scale habitat use by black-footed ferrets (*Mustela nigripes*) released on black-tailed prairie dog (*Cynomys ludovicianus*) colonies in New Mexico: Fort Collins, Colorado State University, master's thesis, 77 p.

Cully, J.F., Johnson, T.L., Collinge, S.K., and Ray, C., 2010, Disease limits populations: plague and black-tailed prairie dogs: Vector-Borne and Zoonotic Diseases, v. 10, no. 1, p. 7–15.

Facka, A.N., Ford, P.L., and Roemer, G.W., 2008, A novel approach for assessing density and range-wide abundance of prairie dogs: Journal of Mammalogy, v. 89, p. 356–364.

Fagerstone, K.A., and Biggins, D.E., 1986, Comparison of capturerecapture and visual count indices of prairie dog (*Cynomys* spp.) densities in blackfooted ferret (*Mustela nigripes*) habitat: Great Basin Naturalist Memoirs, v. 8, p. 94–98.

Fitzgerald, J.P., 1993, The ecology of plague in Gunnison's prairie dogs and suggestions for the recovery of black-footed ferrets, *in* Oldemeyer, J., Biggins, D., Miller, B., and Crete, R., eds., Management of prairie dog complexes for reintroduction of the black-footed ferret: Washington, D.C., U.S. Fish and Wildlife Service, Biological Report 13, p. 50–59.

Godbey, J.L, Biggins, D.E., and Garelle, D., 2006, Exposure of captive black-footed ferrets (*Mustela nigripes*) to plague, *in* Roelle, J.E., Miller, B.J., Godbey, J.L., and Biggins, D.E., eds., Recovery of the black-footed ferret—progress and continuing challenges: U.S. Geological Survey Scientific Investigations Report 2005-5293, p. 233–237.

Hoogland, J.L., 1995, The black-tailed prairie dog—Social life of a burrowing mammal: Chicago, University of Chicago Press, 557 p.

Horvitz, D.G., and Thompson, D.J., 1952, A generalization of sampling without replacement from a finite universe: Journal of the American Statistical Association, v. 47, p. 663–685.

Huggins, R.M., 1991, Some practical aspects of a conditional likelihood approach to capture experiments: Biometrics, v. 47, p. 725–732.

Johnson, W.C., and Collinge, S.K., 2004, Landscape effects on black-tailed prairie dog colonies: Biological Conservation, v. 115, p. 487–497.

Kotliar, N.B., 2000, Application of the new keystone-species concept to prairie dogs—How well does it work?: Conservation Biology, v. 14, p. 1715–1721.

Kotliar, N.B., Miller, B.J., Reading, R.P., and Clark, T.W., 2006, The prairie dog as a keystone species: *in* Hoogland, J.L., ed., Conservation of the black-tailed prairie dog: Washington, D.C., Island Press, p. 53–64.

Lu, D., Mausel, P., Brondizio, E., and Moran, E., 2004, Change detection techniques: International Journal of Remote Sensing, v. 25, p. 2365–2407.

Luce, R.J., ed., 2003, A multi-state conservation plan for the black-tailed prairie dog, *Cynomys ludovicianus*, in the United States—An addendum to the black-tailed conservation assessment and strategy, November 3, 1999, 79 p.

MacKenzie, D.I., Nichols, J.D. , Royle, J.A., Pollock, K.H., Bailey, L.L., and Hines, J.E., 2006, Occupancy estimation and modeling. Burlington, Mass., Elsevier, 344 p.

Manly, B.F.J., 2006, Randomization, bootstrap and Monte Carlo methods in biology (3rd ed.): London, Chapman and Hall, 300 p.

Manly, B.F.J., 2009, Statistics for environmental science and management (2nd ed.): London, Chapman and Hall, 295 p.

Matchett, R.M., Biggins, D.E., Carlson, V., Powell, B., and Rocke, T., 2010, Enzootic plague reduces black-footed ferret (*Mustela nigripes*) survival in Montana: Vector-Borne and Zoonotic Diseases, v. 10, no. 1, p. 27–35.

McDonald, T.L., 2004, GRTS for the average Joe: West, Inc., last accessed March 10, 2011 at *http://www.west-inc.com/reports/grts.pdf*.

McDonald, T.L., Manly, B.F.J., and Nielson, R.M., 2009, Review of environmental monitoring methods—Trend detection: West, Inc., last accessed March 10, 2011 at *http://www.west-inc.com/reports/Review%20of%20Trend%20Detection2009.pdf*.

McDonald, T.L., 2010, MRA—Analysis of mark-recapture data: West, Inc., last accessed March 10, 2011 at *http://cran.r-project.org/web/packages/mra*.

Menkens, Jr., G.E., Biggins, D.E., and Anderson, S.H., 1990, Visual counts as an index of white-tailed prairie dog density: Wildlife Society Bulletin, v. 18, p. 290–296.

Papworth, S.K., Rist, J., Coad, L., and Milner-Gulland, E.J., 2008, Evidence for shifting baseline syndrome in conservation: Conservation Letters, v. 2, p. 93–100.

Powell, K.L., Robel, R.J., Kemp, K.E., and Nellis, M.D., 1994, Aboveground counts of black-tailed prairie dogs—temporal nature and relationship to burrow entrance density: Journal of Wildlife Management, v. 58, p. 361–366.

Proctor, J., Haskins, B., and Forrest, S.C., 2006, Focal areas for conservation of prairie dogs and the grassland ecosystem *in* Hoogland, J.L., ed., Conservation of the black-tailed prairie dog: Washington, D.C., Island Press, p. 232–247.

Seglund, A.E., Ernst, A.E., Grenier, M., Luce, B., Puchniak, A., and Schnurr, P., 2006, White-tailed prairie dog conservation assessment: Laramie, Wyo., Western Association of Fish and Wildlife Agencies, Unpublished Report, 138 p.

Seglund, A.E., Ernst, A.E., and O'Neill, D.M., 2005, Gunnison's prairie dog conservation assessment: Laramie, Wyo., Western Association of Fish and Wildlife Agencies, Unpublished Report, 87 p.

Severson, K.E., and Plumb, G.E., 1998, Comparison of methods to estimate population densities of black-tailed prairie dogs: Wildlife Society Bulletin, v. 26, p. 859–866.

Soulé, M.E., Estes, J.A., Berger, J., and del Río, C.M., 2003, Ecological effectiveness—Conservation goals for interactive species: Conservation Biology, v. 17, p. 1238–1250.

Stalmaster, M.V., 1988, Ferruginous hawk nesting mitigation study: Final Report:Denver, Colo., ERO Resources Corporation, 97 p.

Stevens, D.L., and Olsen, A.R., 2003, Variance estimation for spatially balanced samples of environmental resources: Environmetrics, v. 14, p. 593–610.

Stevens, D.L. and Olsen, A.R., 2004, Spatially balanced sampling of natural resources: Journal of the American Statistical Association, v. 99, p. 262–278.

Theobald, D.M., Stevens, Jr., D.L., White, D., Urquhart, N.S., Olsen, A.R., and Norman, J.B., 2007, Using GIS to generate spatially-balanced random survey designs for natural resource applications: Environmental Management, v. 40, p. 134–146.

U.S. Department of Agriculture, Farm Service Agency, 2009, National Agriculture Imagery Program information sheet: Salt Lake City, Ut., Aerial Photography Field Office, last accessed March 19, 2011 at *http://www.fsa.usda.gov/Internet/FSA_File/naip_2009_info_final.pdf*.

U.S. Department of Interior, 2008, Endangered and threatened wildlife and plants; 12-month finding on a petition to list the Gunnison's prairie dog as threatened or endangered: Federal Register, v. 73, p. 6660-6684.

U.S. Fish and Wildlife Service, 1991, Utah prairie dog recovery plan: Denver, Colo., U.S. Fish and Wildlife Service, 41 p.

U.S. Fish and Wildlife Service, 2010, Utah prairie dog occupancy and habitat survey protocol for Federal section 7 consultations, April 2010: last accessed June 3, 2010, at *http://www.fws.gov/utahfieldoffice/Documents/UPD2010Training/Survey%20Protocol/UPD%20Survey%20Protocol_FINAL_4-13-10.pdf*.

Van Pelt, W.E., ed., 1999, The black-tailed prairie dog conservation assessment and strategy: Phoenix, Arizona Game and Fish Department, Nongame and Endangered Wildlife Program, Technical Report 159, 55 p.

Weltzin, J.F., Archer, S., and Heitschmidt, R.K., 1997, Small-mammal regulation of vegetation structure in a temperate savanna: Ecology, v. 78, p. 751–763.

Western Association of Fish and Wildlife Agencies, 2006, White-tailed prairie dog and Gunnison's prairie dog conservation strategy: Laramie, Wyo, Western Association of Fish and Wildlife Agencies, unpublished report, 23 p.

Western Association of Fish and Wildlife Agencies, 2007, Gunnison's prairie dog conservation plan—Addendum to the white-tailed prairie dog and Gunnison's prairie dog conservation strategy: Laramie, Wyo., Western Association of Fish and Wildlife Agencies, unpublished report, 44 p.

Whicker, A.D., and Detling, J.K., 1988, Ecological consequences of prairie dog disturbances: BioScience, v. 38, p. 778–785.

White, G.C., 2008, Closed population estimation models and their extension in program MARK: Environmental and Ecological Statistics, v. 15, p. 89–99.

White, G.C., and Burnham, K.P., 1999, Program MARK—Survival estimation from populations of marked animals: Bird Study, v. 46 (Supplement), p. S120–S139.

Appendix 1. Workshop Attendee List

NAME	TITLE	AFFILIATION	ADDRESS/PHONE/E-MAIL
Abbott, Tyler	Wildlife Biologist	Bureau of Land Management Wyoming	5353 Yellowstone Road Cheyenne, WY 82003 307-775-6090 tyler.abbott@blm.gov
Ballard, Warren	Faculty	Texas Tech University	Dept of Range, Wildlife, and Fisheries Management Box 52125 Lubbock, TX 79409-2125 806-742-2280 warren.ballard@ttu.edu
Biggins, Dean	Research Wildlife Biologist	U.S. Geological Survey	2150 Centre Avenue, Bldg C Fort Collins, CO 80526 970-226-9467 bigginsd@usgs.gov
Brian, Nancy	Endangered Species Specialist	National Park Service	1201 Oakridge Drive, Ste 200 Fort Collins, CO 80525 970-267-2103 nancy_brian@nps.gov
Bunnell, Kevin D., Ph.D	Mammals Coordinator	Utah Division of Wildlife Resources	1594 W. North Temple Salt Lake City, UT 84114 801-538-4758 kevinbunnell@utah.gov
Castle, Kevin T.	Wildlife Veterinarian	National Park Service	1201 Oakridge Drive, Ste 200 Fort Collins, CO 80525 kevin_castle@nps.gov
Chase, Myron	National Resource Specialist	Intermountain Regional Office, National Park Service	12795 W. Alameda Pkwy Lakewood, CO 80228 303-969-2863 myron_chase@nps.gov
Corcoran, Jeffrey	Wildlife Specialist II	Arizona Game and Fish Department	P O Box 1175 Seligman, AZ 86337 618-559-6131 jcorcoran@azgfd.gov
Cully, Jack F. Ph.D	Asst Unit Leader/ Associate Professor	U.S. Geological Survey	USGS Cooperative Research Unit 204 Leasure Hall Kansas State University Manhattan, KS 66506 785-532-6534 bcully@usgs.gov
Earnhardt, Joanne	Population Biologist	Lincoln Park Zoo	*joanne@lpzoo.org*
Ellison, Laura	Ecologist	U.S. Geological Survey	2150 Centre Avenue. Bldg C Ft. Collins, CO 80526 970-226-9494 ellisonl@usgs.gov
Figueroa, Wendy	Conservation Biologist	Colorado Division of Wildlife	122 E. Edison Brush, CO 80723 970-842-6340 wendy.figueroa@state.co.us
Forrest, Steve	Manager, Restoration Science	World Wildlife Fund – U.S.	302 S. Block St, Ste 5 Bozeman, MT 59715 406-581-2663 steve_forrest@wwfus.org

NAME	TITLE	AFFILIATION	ADDRESS/PHONE/E-MAIL
Gober, Joy	Biologist	U.S. Fish and Wildlife Service, Region 6	420 S. Garfield Ave., Ste 400 Pierre, SD 57501 joy_gober@fws.gov
Gober, Pete	Black-footed Ferret Recovery Coordinator	U.S. Fish and Wildlife Service, Region 6	420 S. Garfield Ave., Ste 400 Pierre, SD 57501 605-224-8693, ext 224 pete_gober@fws.gov
Grassel, Shaun	Wildlife Biologist	Lower Brule Sioux Tribe	P O Box 246 Lower Brule, SD 57548 605-473-5666 *smgrassel@gmail.com*
Grenier, Martin	Non-Game Mammal Biologist	Wyoming Game and Fish Department	260 Buena Vista Drive Lander, WY 82520 307-332-2688 *martin.grenier@wgf.state.wy.us*
Griebel, Randall	Wildlife Biologist	U.S. Forest Service Wall Ranger District	P O Box 425 Wall, SD 57790 605-279-2125 rgriebel@fs fed.us
Hays, Misty	Deputy District Ranger	U.S. Forest Service, Thunder Basin National Grassland	2250 E. Richards Street Douglas, WY 82633 307-358-7102 mahayes@fs fed.us
Hicks, Holly	Deputy District Ranger	Arizona Game and Fish Department	5000 W. Carefree Hwy Phoenix, AZ 85086 623-236-7499 hhicks@asgfd.gov
Hutchins, Michael Ph.D	Executive Director	The Wildlife Society	5410 Grosvenor Lane Bethesda, MD 20814 301-897-9770 *Michael@wildlife.org*
Kempema, Silka L. F.	Terrestrial Wildlife Biologist	South Dakota Dept. of Game, Fish & Parks	523 E. Capitol Avenue Pierre, SD 57501 605-773-2740 *silka.kempema@state.sd.us*
Koprowski, John		University of Arizona	Wildlife and Fisheries Science School of Natural Resources 214 Biological Sciences East University of Arizona Tucson, AZ 85721 520-626-5895 squirrcl@ag.arizona.cdu
Lamb, Lee	Facilitator	Negotiation Guidance Associates	*bleelamb@me.com*
Larson, Scott	Field Supervisor	U.S. Fish and Wildlife Service, Region 6	420 S. Garfield Ave. Pierre, SD 57501 *scott_larson@fws.gov*
Livieri, Travis	Wildlife Biologist	Prairie Wildlife Research	P O Box 308 Wellington, CO 80549 970-219-1659 *tlivieri@prairiewildlife.org*
Lukacs, Paul	Biometrician	Colorado Division of Wildlife	*paul.lukacs@state.co.us*
Maddux, Henry	Program Supervisor	U.S. Fish and Wildlife Service, Region 6	303-236-4251 *henry_maddux@fws.gov*

NAME	TITLE	AFFILIATION	ADDRESS/PHONE/E-MAIL
Marsh, Chris	Habitat Biologist	South Dakota Dept. of Game, Fish & Parks	523 East Capitol Pierre, SD 57501 605-773-2868 *christopher.marsh@state.sd.us*
Martin, Paula		Prairie Ecosystems Assc	
Matchett, Randy	Wildlife Biologist	U.S. Fish and Wildlife Service, Charles M Russell NWR	333 Airport Road Lewistown, MT 59457 406-538-8706 *randy_matchett@fws.gov*
McCain, Lauren	Prairie Protection Director	WildEarth Guardians	1536 Wyncoop St., Ste 301 Denver, CO 80202 303-720-563-9306 *lmccain@wildearthguardians.org*
McDonald, Brandon	Wildlife Biologist	Bureau of Land Management Vernal Field Office	170 S. 500 E Vernal, UT 84078 435-781-4449
McDonald, Lyman	Senior Statistician/Biometrician	Western EcoSystems Technology, Inc	2003 Central Avenue Cheyenne, WY 82001 307-634-1756 *lmcdonald@west-inc.com*
Miller, Sterling Ph.D	Wildlife Biologist	National Wildlife Federation	240 N. Higgins, Ste 2 Missoula, MT 59807 *millers@nwf.org*
Muenchau, Barbara	Biology Tech	Wind Cave National Park, SD	26611 US Highway 385 Hot Springs, SD 57747 605-745-1150 *barbara_muenchau@nps.gov*
Odell, Eric	Species Conservation Coordinator	Colorado Division of Wildlife	317 W. Prospect Ft. Collins, CO 80526 970-472-4340 *eric.odell@state.co.us*
Otis, David	Unit Leader and Collaborating Professor	Iowa State University	USGS Iowa Cooperative Research Unit Department of Natural Resource, Ecology & Management 342 Science II Iowa State University Ames, Iowa 50011-3221 515.294.7639 dotis@iastate.edu
Peek, Matt	Wildlife Biologist	Kansas Department of Wildlife and Parks	P O Box 1525 Emporia, KS 66801 620-342-0658 mattp@wps.state ks.us
Petch, Brad	Wildlife Biologist	Colorado Division of Wildlife	711 Independent Avenue Grand Junction, CO 81505 brad.petch@state.co.us
Pfister, Al	Project Leader	U.S. Fish and Wildlife Service, Western Colorado Office	764 Horizon Drive, Bldg B Grand Junction, CO 81506 al_pfister@fws.gov
Painter, Cristi	Wildlife Biologist	U.S. Forest Service, Thunder Basin National Grassland	2250 E. Richards Street Douglas, WY 82633 cpainter@fs fed.us

NAME	TITLE	AFFILIATION	ADDRESS/PHONE/E-MAIL
Pusateri, Francie	Sr. Wildlife Biologist	Colorado Division of Wild-life	317 W. Prospect Ft. Collins, CO 80526 francie.pusateri@state.co.us
Quamen, Frank	Wildlife Biologist	Bureau of Land Management	Denver Federal Center, Bldg 50 Denver, CO 303-236-6310 *frank_quamen@blm.gov*
Rauscher, Ryan	Wildlife Biologist	Montana Fish, Wildlife and Parks	5478 US Hwy 2W Glasgow, MT 59230 rrauscher@mt.gov
Richardson, Katherine	Fish & Wildlife Biologist	U.S. Fish and Wildlife Service, Region 6	2369 W. Orten Circle, Ste 50 West Valley City, UT 84199 801-975-3330 x 125 *katherine_richardson@fws.gov*
Robertson, Erin		Center for Native Ecosystems	
Roddy, Dan	Biologist	National Park Service, Wind Cave National Park,	26611 US Highway 385 Hot Springs, SD 57747 605-745-1157 *dan_roddy@nps.gov*
Schroeder, Greg	Biologist	National Park Service, Badlands National Park	25216 Ben Reifel Road Interior, SD 57750 *greg_schroeder@nps.gov*
Seglund, Amy	SW Wildlife Conservation Coordinator	Colorado Division of Wild-life	2300 S. Townsend Montrose, CO 81401 970-252-6014 *amy.seglund@state.co.us*
Sidle, John G.		U.S. Forest Service	125 N. Main St Chadron, NE 69337 308-432-0300 *hsudke@fs.fed.ys*
Singhurst, Jason	Botanist	Texas Parks and Wildlife Department	4200 S. School Road Austin, TX 78704 512-389-4800 *jason.singhurst@tpwd.state.tx.us*
Stanley, Tom	Research Wildlife Biologist	U.S. Geological Survey	2150 Centre Avenue, Bldg C Fort Collins, CO 80526 970-226-9360 Stanleyt@usgs.gov
Sterling Krank, Lindsey	Director	The Prairie Dog Coalition, Humane Society of the United States	2525 Arapahoe, #E4-527 Boulder, CO 80302 720-938-0788 *director@prairiedogcoalition.org*
Stevens, Patty	Branch Chief	U.S. Geological Survey	2150 Centre Avenue, Bldg C Fort Collins, CO 80526 970-226-9499 stevensp@usgs.gov
Stuart, James N.		New Mexico Dept Game and Fish	P.O. Box 25112 Santa Fe, NM 87504 505-476-8107 *james.stuart@state.nm.us*
Sweikert, Lily	Wildlife Biologist	Turner Endangered Species Fund	28044 Bad River Road Fort Pierre, SD 57532 605-222-6258 *lily.sweikert@retronches.com*

NAME	TITLE	AFFILIATION	ADDRESS/PHONE/E-MAIL
Tripp, Dan	Wildlife Disease Researcher	Colorado Division of Wildlife	317 W. Prospect Ft. Collins, CO 80526 970-472-4478 *dan.tripp@state.co.us*
Van Pelt, Bill	Grassland Coordinator	WAFWA Grassland Coordinator	5000 W. Carefree Hwy Phoenix, AZ 85086 623-236-7573 bvanpelt@asgfd.gov
Weimers, Larry	Biologist	Oklahoma Dept of Wildlife Conservation	5705 Major Road Freedom, OK 73842 405-990-7206 *lweimers@sbcglobd.net*
White, Gary C.	Professor Emeritus	Colorado State University	Department of Fish, Wildlife, and Conservation Biology Fort Collins, CO 80523 970-491-6678 *gwhite@cnr.colostate.edu*
Wrede, John	Biologist	National Park Service, Northern Great Plains Inventory and Monitoring Network	231 E. St. Joe St. Rapid City, SD 57701 605-341-2805 *jwrede@nps.gov*

Appendix 2. Homework Questions

1. What parameters are you trying to estimate?

2. What is your target population?

3. What is your sample unit and how is it defined?

4. How did you construct your sampling frame?

5. What was your sampling design?

6. What methods were used to account imperfect detectability (i.e., estimate detection probability)?

7. What analytical methodology or models are being used to turn data into parameter estimates (and their error estimates)?

8. Given you agree that data from multiple sources (for example, States) should be aggregated to assess prairie dog status rangewide, what do you think the target population should be and what parameters do you think should be estimated for that target population?

9. How do the monitoring objectives you presented, specifically the parameters you are estimating and the target population you are estimating these parameters for (that is, questions 1 and 2 above), fit in to the overarching objective (that is, the "target population") you specified in the last question (question 8)?

10. What were the costs to conduct your survey methodology?

Appendix 3. The Need for Prairie Dog Conservation Activities on Focal Areas

Although beyond the charge to the panel and not part of the panel's recommendations for this workshop, we think the use of conservation focal areas as discussed in the MSCP would be beneficial if extended to all four species of prairie dogs in the United States. Management and monitoring options on conservation focal areas should address questions of ecological functioning that will allow more refined goals to be set for future conservation efforts.

Important functions of prairie dogs as a keystone (Kotliar, 2000) and foundation (Soulé and others, 2003) species are linked to their densities and abundance (Kotliar and others, 2006). We acknowledge the economic constraints to obtaining reliable density estimates for prairie dogs across multiple States but feel that it is essential to emphasize the link between many ecosystem functions of prairie dogs and population attributes, such as density and stability. Threats to those population attributes are not always closely tied to threats that might reduce colony coverage or distribution of prairie dogs.

Ecosystem functions of prairie dogs include their roles as prey, ecosystem engineers, and modifiers of the vegetative community. Dependency on prairie dogs as prey is epitomized by the endangered black-footed ferret (*Mustela nigripes*). Relatively high prairie dog densities likely are required for reproduction by ferrets (Biggins and others, 1993). Similarly, ferruginous hawk (*Buteo regalis*) nesting success plummeted with declines of prairie dog and lagomorph populations in western Colorado (Stalmaster, 1988). The role of prairie dogs as ecosystem engineers is defined mostly by their construction of deep and complex burrow systems that provide habitat for associated species, such as burrowing owls (*Athene cunicularia*) and result in soil mixing. Prairie dogs also alter the vegetative cover on their colonies, with a variety of consequences (Whicker and Detling, 1988), and their importance in maintaining grasslands and reducing shrub encroachment likely has been understated (Weltzin and others,1997). In order to maintain these functions and others within at least part of the historic ranges of prairie dogs, the concept of focal areas for prairie dog conservation was developed. For the BTPD, these areas were defined as complexes or potential complexes (clusters of colonies separated by ≤7 km) having >1000 acres occupied by prairie dogs, with each State having at least 1 complex with >5,000 occupied acres (Luce, 2003). Proctor and others (2006) suggest 4,000 ha (9,884 ac) as being a more effective minimum considering requirements of black-footed ferrets. At present, there is not an explicit goal for prairie dog density on focal areas, although a minimum density of 10 prairie dogs per acre (25 per hectare) is implied by the definition of "colony" for black-tailed prairie dogs (Luce, 2003). Most focal areas at present emphasize black-footed ferret management, but the potential for ferret reintroduction should not be regarded as the only justification for maintaining large blocks of habitat with high densities of prairie dogs. Although ferrets

serve as a flagship species driving prairie dog conservation in many areas, we believe that other values and keystone functions of prairie dogs (for example, creating nesting areas for burrowing owls, and so on) provide sufficient justification for establishment of focal areas at sites that might not be conducive (biologically or socially) to reintroduction of ferrets.

A century ago, we might have been able to assume that maintaining a broad distribution of prairie dogs with some relatively large focal areas also would assure that many of the ecological functions of prairie dogs would be concomitant. The validity of that assumption became questionable after introduction of plague (caused by the bacterium *Yersinia pestis*) to North America. Although plague alone might not presently be threatening any prairie dog species with imminent extinction, the disease is modifying the ecological function of prairie dogs (Seglund, 2005a, b). Some threats of plague are mentioned in the conservation strategy for the BTPD (Luce, 2003), the conservation assessment for the WTPD (Seglund and others, 2005a), the conservation assessment for the GUPD (Seglund and others, 2005b), and the recovery plan for the UTPD (United States Fish and Wildlife Service, 1991). More recent information highlights additional threats that were not mentioned in those documents.

Within prairie dog systems, plague can have dramatic and easily noticeable effects by causing epizootics that result in massive dieoffs of prairie dogs. These epizootic cycles result in population oscillations that were unlikely to have been historically characteristic of prairie dogs (Biggins and Kosoy, 2001). Although Hoogland (1995) characterized the apparently plague-free Wind Cave National Park population of BTPDs he studied as having significant annual variation, that variation was minor when compared to variation in the population at the Rocky Mountain Arsenal, a site with recurrent epizootics of plague. Using Hoogland's (1995) 14 years of data for Wind Cave, the coefficient of variation (CV) for the population was 13 percent compared to a CV of 96 percent for 14 years of colony coverage data at the Rocky Mountain Arsenal. Although the CV does not adequately describe the temporally autocorrelated data of these population cycles, it serves as an index to the relative variability of these two populations. Epidemiological theory links disease transmission rates to density of host organisms. If transmission rates for plague follow a typically density-dependent pattern (Barnes, 1993), epizootics become increasingly likely as prairie dog populations increase. However, large populations of prairie dogs are those that best support reproduction of species such as black-footed ferrets and ferruginous hawks. Thus, the population peaks of prey that might once have created the boom years for these species may now be subdued due to plague, and the presumably depressed mean population levels could be commonly lower than the thresholds necessary to support reproduction by these species.

Plague also can produce substantial effects without causing catastrophic population collapses. Two recent studies suggest that plague is having large impacts on BTPDs, WTPDs, GUPDs, and black-footed ferrets, even when it does not erupt into epizootic form. During a 5-year prairie dog study in Utah and Montana, plague was managed by reducing flea vectors on some plots but not others. Survival of adult prairie dogs was 31-45 percent higher on plots with flea control compared to nonmanaged plots (Biggins and others, 2010). At a study site in Montana, ferret survival was assessed under a design with 4 treatments involving colonies with and without flea control and ferrets that were vaccinated or not vaccinated for plague. Flea control or the experimental plague vaccine improved annual ferret survival by >200 percent, and there was a significant interaction suggesting nonadditive effects of the two treatments (Matchett and others, 2010). Unlike the flea control treatment which could induce effects by controlling ectoparasites and other vector-borne diseases, the vaccine was specific for plague. Thus, the ferret experiment precludes explanations other than plague, and the 5-year experiment with prairie dogs demonstrated how widespread the phenomenon might be. During those studies, plague was rarely detected using common diagnostic tests on hundreds of potential rodent hosts and thousands of their fleas at those study sites, illustrating that low detection rates or even lack of detection do not imply low risk to wildlife populations. Ferret populations at the Montana study site have not been self-sustaining without plague-management intervention. Further, the prairie dog study suggested that these chronic mortality rates in prairie dogs likely hamper prairie dog population growth rates (although low survival was not always associated with population decline) and suggested that other demographic parameters were altered (Biggins and others, 2010). The two studies collectively imply that effects of enzootic plague can be amplified at higher trophic levels. Ferrets and prairie dogs probably are similarly susceptible to the disease (90+ percent mortality compared to ~50 percent mortality in untreated human cases), but vulnerability of ferrets could be increased because of their longer movements and exposure through infected carrion (Godbey and others, 2006).

WTPDs are notably vulnerable to chronic effects of enzootic plague. Evidence of plague was found during 10 of the 11 years in which surveys were done at the Meeteetse, Wyoming complex of WTPDs during 1985-2008. The estimated prairie dog population declined during 1988-1993, recovered somewhat between 1997 and 2008 (United States Geological Survey, unpublished data), but did not reach the level recorded during 1985. Similarly, WTPDs had low survival rates associated with intermittent detection of plague during a 5-year study in eastern Utah (Biggins and others, 2010). There seems to be no reliable baseline data on population densities for any of the white-tail subgenus (WTPD, GUPD, UTPD) prior to the invasion of plague into their habitats [much of the invasion likely occurred during the 1930s and 1940s (Fitzgerald, 1993)].

Populations of GUPDs and UTPDs appear to have been locally extirpated owing to plague, and the disease has been recognized as a threat sufficient to warrant listing of GUPDs at high elevations (United States Department of Interior, 2008). The white-tailed subgenus is often characterized as having patchy distributions of populations at low densities, but we cannot assess whether this phenomenon was historically normal, or a result of decades of chronic plague. Our perceptions of normalcy for these prairie dogs might be another example of the shifting baseline syndrome associated with the general amnesia of passing human generations (Papworth and others, 2008). On the other hand, it is possible that dispersed low-density populations of these species were always common and widespread, and that plague is only a minor perturbation of that theme.

Thus, especially for the white-tailed subgenus, lack of historical baseline data prevents a realistic assessment of the impact plague has had on ecological functioning of prairie dog communities and likewise hinders establishment of realistic conservation goals. Now, the only way to gain insight into historical relationships will be to remove plague from complexes of prairie dogs at relatively large scales of space (1000s of acres) and time (10s of years), and monitor their populations, populations of associated species, and other community attributes. Setting up such a large-scale plan to produce interpretable results should involve plague-managed complexes and paired "control" complexes where plague is not manipulated, accompanied by relatively intensive monitoring, and should involve replication over at least several sites. Although this project has elements of experimental research, we believe the scales of space and time, financial commitments, and operational management implications suggest a cooperative venture involving conservation organizations, land-management agencies, wildlife-management agencies, and established research institutions. We offer suggestions below for the establishment of such a project if the State and Federal agencies judge that it is justified, feasible and if funding can be secured.

For BTPD communities within the present range of plague, the suite of questions regarding ecological function is similar to those discussed above. Cully and others, (2010), for example, noted that plague regulates BTPD populations and distribution on the landscape. Because there are complexes of BTPD colonies in areas where plague has not been documented, there is an opportunity to compare some of the functions of apparently plague-free populations with those impacted by plague. That opportunity is compromised by confounding factors, however. Plague-free populations are in the easterly portion of the BTPD range and plague-affected populations are in the westerly portion of the range; climate and elevation differ, and these factors likely affect population densities. Coupled with these varying influences are differences in agricultural development that have led to different levels of fragmentation, and consequently, to differing wildlife communities. Thus, gaining an improved understanding of ecological function for western BTPDs might again be attainable only with broad-scale manipulations of plague. Alternatively, a recent invasion of plague into BTPD complexes in South Dakota allows something of a longitudinal case study on effects of plague. Large datasets were collected on the expansive BTPD complex of Conata Basin/Badlands National Park (~26,000 acres) prior to the invasion of plague in 2008. Management of plague and continued data collection provide a unique opportunity to gain insight into the effects of plague on ecological function for eastern BTPDs.

General recommendations:

1. In WTPD and GUPD conservation strategies, include conservation focal areas conceptually similar to those described in the BTPD conservation strategy. Assure that there is a representative mix of high and middle elevation GUPD complexes as focal areas in Arizona, Colorado, New Mexico, and Utah.

2. Add a conservation focal-area component to the UTPD recovery plan, or perhaps add three of these so there will be one suitable focal area in each of the West Desert, Paunsaugunt, and Awapa Recovery Areas.

3. Within the range of plague, manage plague on complexes that are conservation focal areas and randomly pair these with similar complexes that that have no plague management to serve as control sites. There should be at least one pair of these focal areas per State per species. Again, the plague-managed focal areas should be regarded at this point primarily as a tool to gain a better understanding of historical functioning of prairie dog communities without plague. The numbers of sites recommended establishes a minimum level if management and monitoring strategies are the same among States so that data results can be cooperatively exchanged, analyzed, and reported. Under this plan, there would be 4 pairs of sites for GUPDs, 3 pairs of sites of WTPDs, and 3 pairs of sites for UTPDs. If plague management and monitoring are well-coordinated among States, these 10 pairs of sites might be assessed collectively for subgenus-level attributes. This plan would call for 4-10 plague managed focal areas for BTPDs, depending on choices by States with BTPD ranges bisected by the current range of plague.

4. Monitor prairie dog densities on these focal areas and their controls. Monitor associated species of high interest (especially predators of prairie dogs). We hesitate to recommend specific monitoring protocols here, but for prairie dogs, methods could include monitoring burrow densities (Biggins and others, 1993) as a coarse index to densities of prairie dogs (extensive coverage with relatively low expense) coupled with subsampling of plots using visual counts (Menkens and others, 1990), capture-mark-recapture techniques (Fagerstone and Biggins, 1986), or capture-mark-reobserve techniques (Facka and others, 2008).

5. East of the range of plague, institute at least a low level of prairie dog density monitoring on focal areas for BTPDs, and do serological monitoring of carnivores to check systematically for presence of plague. If plague is detected, institute plague management and higher levels of monitoring suggested above.

6. After each 5-year period, collectively evaluate the data from plague-managed and nonmanaged focal areas, and establish future management and monitoring levels. Consider ongoing developments regarding tools for plague management.

7. Because of the learning objectives associated with managed conservation focal areas, prairie dog shooting should not be allowed in these areas, and livestock grazing should be carefully managed.

As implied in the BTPD conservation strategy (Luce, 2003, p.18), it seems futile to further pursue the concepts of reserve design and long-term viability for any prairie dog species until there is a better understanding of prairie dog systems where plague is managed. Thus, these recommendations emphasize gaining that understanding and setting a foundation for future goals. This is a long-term process; quick results should not be expected. Some responses might be subtle and confounded by interactions of other responses. For example, if population growth rates for prairie dogs tend to be improved by plague management, there could be functional and numerical responses by predators that dampen those rates. Hence, there is a need for a systems approach to monitoring.

Ultimately, plague management could involve prophylactic treatments (vaccine or vector control) or plague monitoring and a response plan when epizootic plague is imminent. Learning more about causes of plague cycles and effects of enzootic levels of plague, and about causes for epizootic eruptions of the disease, will help determine which management scenarios are most pragmatic. We propose prophylactic treatment as the best option for learning about the collective effects of both chronic and epizootic plague.

Appendix 4. National Agriculture Imagery Program Overview

The USDA's Farm Service Agency (FSA) directs the National Agriculture Imagery Program (commonly known by the acronym NAIP) to provide 'leaf-on' digital ortho photographic imagery during the growing season to governmental agencies, affiliates, and the public within a year of acquisition and often much less. Direct administration of the program is through the Aerial Photography Field Office in Salt Lake City, Utah. NAIP imagery products have several strengths: (1) wide availability, (2) broad coverage, (3) sufficient resolution, (4) ease of acquisition, (5) past imagery for pilot projects and comparisons, (6) cost (typically free of charge), and (7) likely future availability of multiband data (red, green, blue, and near infrared).

NAIP imagery is digital and of high resolution (a 1-m ground sample distance) and has a horizontal accuracy of <6 m. Current imagery is provided in natural color consisting of 3 bands (red, green, blue), but near infrared also is being made available. Contractual obligations require that cloud cover must be ≤10 percent and imagery is inspected for visual quality and horizontal accuracy by using known points under the direction of the Aerial Photography Field Office. Imagery products from NAIP typically are available free of charge and are easily downloaded or requested on CD for shipment by mail (links provided below). Beginning in 2009, the program committed to a 3-year cycle of acquisition so that all States will be guaranteed regular coverage on a regular cycle conducive to planning and budgeting.

NAIP imagery is produced in two formats: (1) digital ortho quarter quad tiles (DOQQs), and (2) compressed county mosaics (CCM). Each individual image tile within the mosaic covers a 3.75 x 3.75 minute quarter quadrangle plus a 300 m buffer on all sides. DOQQs are geotiffs, and the area corresponds to the USGS topographic quadrangles. These DOQQs are made available within a year after completion of an entire project area that usually consists of an entire State. CCMs are generated by compressing digital ortho quarter quadrangle image tiles into a single mosaic. The mosaic may cover all or portions of an individual final product and become available in the much shorter time frame of 30-60 days through free download. All individual tile images and the resulting mosaic are rectified in the UTM coordinate system, NAD 83, and cast into a single predetermined UTM zone. CCMs with four bands were compressed into a .jp2 format and are delivered with a "seamline" shapefile delineating detailed image-swath composition of each image.

Access to imagery is facilitated by online nodes for download. CCMs are available for free download through the USDA Geospatial Data Gateway, http://datagateway nrcs.usda.gov/. DOQQs will be mailed to government cooperators after prior arrangement.

The following additional information is available online:

General products, *http://www.fsa.usda.gov/FSA/apfoapp? area=home&subject=prog&topic=nai*

Past coverage (scroll over the State abbreviation on this interactive map), *http://www.fsa.usda.gov/Internet/FSA_File/ naip_coverage03-09.pdf*

Introductory powerpoint presentation, *http://www.fsa. usda.gov/Internet/FSA_File/about_apfo_imagery_srvcs. ppt#286,1,FSA?s%20GIS%20Activities%20at%20the%20%20 Aerial%20Photography%20Field%20Office%20(APFO)*

Appendix 5. Use of Aerial Imagery to Map Features (Potential Prairie Dog Colonies)

Aerial photography has been used for locating and mapping BTPD colonies for many years (summarized by Biggins and others, 2006). The availability of National Agriculture Imagery Program (NAIP) digital photos in natural color (and sometimes color infrared) with 1-2 meter resolution, facilitates a pragmatic method for acquiring data on distribution of prairie dogs over large areas. Photos also have the advantage of providing a permanent record of features existing at a point in time. Images should be archived to allow the flexibility of reinterpretation if criteria and technologies change. The primary problems involved in creating maps of prairie dog colonies from aerial photographs fall into three categories (Biggins and others, 2006). First, the process of distinguishing prairie dog colonies from other features can be problematic. Second, defining perimeters of colonies is inexact. Third, photos provide little information on presence of live prairie dogs. Because of these problems, we recommended the use of double observers to account for features that were not detected followed by aerial and ground surveys of identified features to derive an estimate of occupied acres. We are unable to present a rigid set of criteria that will remove subjectivity from the process of identifying prairie dog colonies on aerial photographs, but present ideas that might improve photo-interpretation consistency. Careful consideration of sources of variation at this preliminary stage can result in greater efficiency of the subsequent aerial- and ground-survey stages.

Prairie dog colonies often are identified on aerial photographs by presence of two attributes used alone or in combination. Although individual burrow entrances are visible only on photographs of the highest resolution (not on standard NAIP images), mounds of soil created by BTPDs when they excavate burrows usually are sufficiently large to register on NAIP images. The other attribute of prairie dog colonies that often is distinctive is the "clip zone" of very short vegetation on colonies compared to surrounding areas. Searches on the ground at times reveal mounds and non-mounded burrows not visible on aerial photos because the burrows are in tall vegetation beyond the clip zone (Biggins and others, 2006). Thus, use of mounds alone to circumscribe prairie dog colonies on aerial photos may result in interpretation of a colony area that is smaller than the area derived from ground survey-based mapping using mounds. Circumscribing the clip zone on the photo often will produce an intermediate area of coverage. The preferred method might depend in part on how one chooses to define a prairie dog colony (for example, the area encompassing all prairie dog use or just the highly used areas) and in part on how one chooses to assess the degree of use by prairie dogs (the area of highly modified vegetation, or the area populated by well-defined burrow systems). For our purposes, precision

would benefit from standardizing the definition and method of assessment.

We might be tempted to standardize on defining a colony as the area of high use by prairie dogs that is delineated by connecting the outermost mounds visible on an aerial photo (Biggins and others, 2006). However, mounds are variably distinguishable within and among photos. At times, their color and contrast match that of the surrounding soil and vegetation. Distinguishing clip zones is arguably more variable than distinguishing mounds because vegetation likely varies even more than soil in color and tonal contrast. Vegetation varies by species, growth conditions, and grazing.

In summary, anything that affects photographic color contrast and tonal contrast of mounds and vegetation on and off a colony can affect our ability to distinguish mounds and clip zones. The following list is not exhaustive but exemplifies the variables:

1. Plant species composition (mound versus non-mound on colony and colony versus non-colony).

2. Grazing pressure by livestock and other ungulates (height of vegetation).

3. Surface soil color and tone (mound contrast with vegetation, bare ground).

4. Subsurface soil color and tone (mounds can contrast with surface soil if they consist of differently colored subsurface soil).

5. Vegetation color and tone (on and off colony, mound soil versus vegetation off mound.

6. Prairie dog population density/activity (grazing affects vegetation height and composition, percentage bare ground).

7. Age of colony (bare ground, vegetation composition).

8. Precipitation (color and tone of soil changes after recent rainfall).

9. Season (plant phenology).

10. Weather patterns (for example, patterns of low versus high precipitation, resulting in variable vegetation).

11. Light quality at time of photo exposure.

12. Light angle at time of photo exposure (low angle produces high shadow contrast and sense of relief; high angle gives flat light).

Features that resemble clip zones and prairie dog mounds can cause additional confusion. Unfortunately, some of these phenomena can be arranged in ways that closely resemble the photographic signatures of prairie dog colonies. These include rocks, patches of alkali soil, and ant hills that can be clustered like prairie dog mounds. Vegetative ecotones resulting from patchy ungulate grazing and transitions among plant species can mimic the clip zones of prairie dog colonies. For these reasons, a combination of clip zone and burrow mounds is a more reliable indicator of prairie dog colonies than either one alone.

Despite the variation caused by a multitude of interacting factors, the fact that prairie dog colonies have been repeatedly mapped from aerial photos and confirmed with data collected on the ground illustrates that the situation is not hopeless. It would be presumptive of us to attempt to dictate criteria, but practitioners would be ill-advised to ignore the potential problems. To reduce variation, we suggest that photointerpreters attempt to standardize criteria that work most of the time for most of the observers and allow truthing data to correct for error that remains. Cumulative evidence suggests that the errors can be both small and estimable.

After features are outlined on the NAIP imagery and ground surveys are completed, complexes of colonies can be circumscribed to meet Objectives 3-5 of the MSCP. Perimeters of such complexes are established by connecting the outer boundaries of colonies that are separated by ≤7 km (that is, the 7 km rule). The procedure is as follows (adapted from Biggins and others, 1993).

1. Start at the northernmost point of the northernmost colony.

2. Pivot a line segment representing 7 km clockwise from grid north until it touches a point on a colony. The line between the first point and the second point begins to define the perimeter of the complex.

3. If a 7-km line segment cannot be pivoted to another colony or portion of the same colony without bisecting the colony perimeter, move clockwise around that colony's perimeter until Step 2 can be accomplished. A convex perimeter of a colony can thus become a segment of the boundary of the complex.

4. Continue to apply Steps 2-3 until the polygon becomes closed.

5. Complexes can be reduced in size by selecting perimeter colonies separated by <7 km (but the 7-km criterion cannot be exceeded). For example, reduction in size might be warranted if a complex would extend into areas where management of the conservation area is not possible or if the complex would be bisected by a barrier that precludes movements of prairie dogs.

Appendix 6. Ground Survey Procedure for Identifying Activity of Colonies

Abundance of burrows often has been used as an index to the abundance of their inhabitants, but we caution that previous studies of this relationship have produced variable results. A significant positive correlation between densities of occupied burrows and prairie dogs was estimated for WTPDs (Biggins and others, 1993) and BTPDs (Biggins and others, 1993, Johnson and Collinge, 2004, Chipault, 2010) although others have failed to detect such a relationship (Powell and others, 1994, Severson and Plumb, 1998). Although it is intuitive that a positive correlation exists because prairie dogs are notably burrowing mammals and occupied prairie dog burrows cannot exist without prairie dogs (recently present, at least), we do not suggest that statistically valid inferences regarding population abundance can be extrapolated from our survey methods. Our primary purpose for assessing prairie dog burrows will be to estimate the proportion of a sampled colony on which prairie dogs recently were present. Because catastrophic losses of prairie dogs due to poisoning or plague can happen quickly (weeks or even days), and scat can appear relatively fresh for somewhat longer periods of time, the term recent implies occupancy within the past couple of months.

We propose use of strip transects to sample densities of burrow openings (occupied and unoccupied) on colonies selected for ground truthing. Before completing these activities, it will be necessary to determine the colonies to be sampled (see discussion elsewhere in this document) and secure permission to access private lands. Sampling of BTPD burrows usually has been done during 1 June–30 September, after young prairie dogs are above ground. Although weather patterns can affect results, sampling should not be inordinately sensitive to minor variations in prairie dog activity due to weather during this spring-summer period. However, long spells of extreme drought and periods of extreme thunderstorm activity should be avoided. The former might cause reduced activity in prairie dogs and flooding during the latter can destroy or re-distribute scat.

The following points are adapted from transect procedures described by Biggins and others (1993):

1. A prairie dog burrow opening is defined as an opening of diameter ≥ 7 cm with a tunnel extending beyond view. Large, badger-reamed burrows are included because prairie dogs often continue to use these burrows after the badger departs.

2. A burrow is classified as occupied if it has fresh scat within 0.5 m of the opening. Fresh scat is defined as droppings that are not dried hard and bleached white but are greenish black or dark brown.

3. Strip transects are 6 meters in width, with length to be determined (see earlier section). The width is maintained by an operator (on foot or on an ATV) carrying a piece of tubing (for example, PVC or electrical conduit) that is 6 meters long.

4. Operator should record the coordinates of begin and end points of each transect, and each burrow opening is coded as occupied or unoccupied. Some States may elect to record a way point for each burrow encountered.

5. If coordinates of all burrow openings are to be recorded (as noted above), operator should carry a GPS receiver capable of saving way points and at least one associated data code (occupied or unoccupied). Otherwise, the starting and ending points of transects can simply be read from simple GPS receivers and recorded on paper forms with total counts of occupied and unoccupied burrows.

6. Operator determines course direction and picks a corresponding landmark far ahead (something on the horizon or at least several kilometers away). Concentration is maintained on the navigation landmark rather than on burrow openings in the vicinity of the observer or immediately ahead. Peripheral vision is used to determine when to stop and examine a burrow opening for inclusion (that is, when more than half the burrow opening is inside the end of the bar). The long, narrow plots have a great deal of edge, so extreme care must be used to avoid biasing the decision regarding inclusion of burrow openings. Avoid letting any burrow opening influence direction of travel, and lay the bar on the ground (if hand-carrying the bar) before looking carefully at any burrow near the edge, making the determination after the bar is stationary. This procedure sounds onerous and time consuming, but close calls will not be common, and a rapid pace usually is easy to maintain. Routinely, 10-15 km of transects can be completed per person per day.

The above steps describe collection of quantitative information. Also collect qualitative notes on observations of digging, plugged burrows, burrows with spider webs, prairie dogs seen (dead or alive), clipped vegetation, evidence of poisoning (flagging, bait remnants, soil shoveled into burrows), and mounds with crusted soil. Collect any dead prairie dogs that are intact if evidence of shooting or poisoning is lacking (send these for plague testing; see collection procedure in BTPD conservation strategy).